When Love Hurts

Reading this book can change your life...by changing the way you love. It will teach you the art of nurturing and caring—the vital powers for survival. You'll discover...

- **Love that Hurts:** How pain grows and thrives in love relationships

- **Changing the Unchangeable:** A new way to look at, and act, in your love relationships

- **Parallels:** How we learn what to expect from past relationships

- **A Different Kind of Love:** Changing the way you care through nurturing

- **The Powers for Survival:** A program that will change your life.

When Love Hurts
Changing the Way You Care

Kenneth M. Piazza, M.D.
with Francine Malder, Ph.D.

Illustrated by Jerry Newman

ACROPOLIS BOOKS LTD.
WASHINGTON, D.C.

for Jack and Pearl who started it all . . .

for Ken and Kris who have to live it . . .

and for Janet who finished it.

©Copyright 1984 Acropolis Books Ltd. All rights reserved. Except for the inclusion of brief quotations in a review, no part of this book may be reproduced or utilized in any form or by any means, electronic or mechanical, including photocopying, recording or by any information storage and retrieval system, without permission in writing from the publisher.

Printed in the United States of America by
COLORTONE PRESS
Creative Graphics, Inc.
Washington, D.C. 20009

Library of Congress Cataloging in Publication Data
Piazza, Kenneth M., 1945—
   When love hurts.
   Bibliography: p.
   Includes index.
   1. Love—Psychological aspects. 2. Change (Psychology). 3. Happiness. I. Title. II. Malder, Francine.
BF575.L8P53   158.'2.   84-6208
ISBN 0-87491-739-5

ACROPOLIS BOOKS, LTD.
Colortone Building, 2400 17th St., N.W.,
Washington, D.C. 20009

Attention: Schools and Corporations
ACROPOLIS books are available at quantity discounts with bulk purchase for educational, business, or sales promotional use. For information, please write to: SPECIAL SALES DEPARTMENT, ACROPOLIS BOOKS LTD., 2400 17th ST., N.W., WASHINGTON, D.C. 20009.

Are there Acropolis Books you want but cannot find in your local stores?
You can get any Acropolis book title in print. Simply send title and retail price, plus 50 cents per copy to cover mailing and handling costs for each book desired. District of Columbia residents add applicable sales tax. Enclose check or money order only, no cash please, to: ACROPOLIS BOOKS LTD., 2400 17th ST., N.W., WASHINGTON, D.C. 20009.

ACKNOWLEDGMENTS

We would like to thank the fine people at Acropolis Books, Ltd. for their support and excellent critiquing of this book. The complex subject matter and pressing time schedules made the support and encouragement of Al Hackl, Kathleen Hughes and Sandy Trupp well received.

We also would like especially to thank Leo Pillot, who throughout his life has done more for the people he's helped than they'll ever know. We know what he's done for the promotion of this book and we thank him.

The original drawings in this book are by Jerry Newman, Professor of Art at Lamar University, Beaumont, Texas. To him, and to Robert Hickey at Acropolis, thanks for making this book so visually beautiful.

Kenneth Piazza
Francine Malder

Introduction 9

Part I

Chapter 1: *Perspectives* 17
Chapter 2: *Patterns* 25
Chapter 3: *Changing* 31
Chapter 4: *A Framework for Loving* 37

Part II

Chapter 5: *Newcomers* 45
Chapter 6: *The Actors* 51
Chapter 7: *The Script* 59
Chapter 8: *New Beginnings* 65
Chapter 9: *Storm and Calm* 71
Chapter 10: *A New Christmas Story* 79

Part III

Chapter 11: *The Survival Plan* 85
Chapter 12: *The Love Debt* 107
Chapter 13: *The Romantic Ideal* 125
Chapter 14: *Play-Acting* 137
Chapter 15: *The Essence of Nurturing and Caring* 153

Appendix 163
Suggested Further Reading 171
Index 173

INTRODUCTION

When Love Hurts

If love has so far brought you pain and anguish, you are not alone. I have, in the course of my work, met thousands of patients who have experienced hurt in love relationships. I would like to share with you my program for healing through *nurturing*.

I've written *When Love Hurts* for everyone who has ever known love *and* pain. It is not a study in abnormal psychology. Rather, it is addressed to all lovers: women and men, children and parents, companions and friends.

Why does love, the greatest of human emotions, hurt so many people? It is a complicated question, but I can begin to answer it by saying that love hurts when we are "caring" in the wrong way.

We first learn to relate to others by watching our parent-figures interact with us and with each other. Based on these early impressions, we formulate patterns of loving that affect us throughout our lives. In keeping with these patterns, we go through life identifying people with familiar roles and expecting them to behave accordingly. Yet, some of the patterns may have been wrong from the start. Others that had

Introduction

sound origins may have unfortunate consequences when replayed in totally different situations.

We, or the ones we love, may have learned to follow the wrong patterns, to "care" in ways that cause hurt. But we can change that.

In this book we'll consider three specific concepts of our emotional selves—based on unconscious habits of thought—that influence the way we care. All three stem largely from childhood experiences. They are, in brief:

- **The Survival Plan:** Our personal strategy for facing up to the rigors, pitfalls, and challenges of life.
- **The Love Debt:** The "wrong" we feel must redress, based on our perception of inequality in the relationship between our parents.
- **The Romantic Ideal:** Our expectations of romantic love, based largely on fantasy.

Combined, these three concepts form a structure that I call the "Love Pyramid."

Although the harmful preconceptions we form early in life are very powerful, they can be changed. Time and again I have been able to help patients break emotional chains and enrich their lives. The essence of my prescription is this: I ask them to perform acts of nurturing that on the surface seem to have little to do with their love relationships.

What is nurturing?

- It is an act of compassion and empathy, a reaching out to others without pity or self-sacrifice.
- It is a state of mind in which distinctions between ally and enemy, predator and victim, no longer exist.
- In the rather special sense in which I am using the word, it is an active involvement with someone or something beyond the self and the small circle of one's family and friends.

I am not able to tell you with authority that humans alone perform acts of nurturance outside this small circle. But our perception of ourselves as nurturing creatures is one of the ways in which we define our humanity.

It may be difficult at first to see any very compelling connection between an act of nurturance performed outside your home, perhaps in the service of someone you do not know well, and the contentment you seek in a personal relationship. But let's approach the matter indirectly.

Try to remember a day when everything went right for you—when you were in fine health, when your work brought immense satisfaction, when the people you loved were accepting and caring. What were you feeling toward the world on that day? I've asked a number of acquaintances, and here are some typical replies:

- "I wanted everyone else to feel as happy as I did."
- "I wanted to sing out to all those gloomy-faced people riding to work on the bus every morning with their noses buried in their newspapers, and say: 'HEY! WAKE UP! Life can be beautiful!'"
- "I wanted to be nice to someone—it didn't matter who—and for once I didn't care if anyone thanked me."

It is hardly surprising that the deep happiness that comes from a satisfying love relationship makes you feel that you want to help others. It should not be surprising, then, that the opposite may also be true—that an approach to life based on nurturing and caring may actually promote happiness in love.

Now, let's try another experiment. Think of a day when you felt tired and depressed, when you quarreled with someone you loved, or discovered that the work you had been doing with care and pride was neither recognized nor valued. Suppose someone approached you that day and asked for a favor that went beyond the normal expectations of friendship. Chances are you'd either refuse or agree very grudgingly.

When we are happy, nurturing comes easily. Let me ask you to consider another possibility: before any of us can be fully contented in a love relationship, we need to develop a true generosity of spirit.

I am reminded of a story by Carson McCullers called "A Tree. A Rock. A Cloud." It takes place on a dark, rainy morning; a handful of people sit hunched over their coffee in a dingy cafe. An unfamiliar man appears, apparently out of nowhere, places his hand on the shoulder of a young paper boy, and announces: "I love you."

The boy is bewildered and uneasy. The adults respond with mocking laughter. But the stranger stands his ground and insists that he has a story to relate.

The man goes on to tell of a much younger woman whom he loved compulsively during almost two years of marriage. (He has, in fact, counted the days and hours.) Then she up and left him.

At first the man was devastated by the loss. Then, gradually, something miraculous happened. As his obsession with this woman faded, the man began to realize that he had set out to love without ever learning how. He had seen his beloved not as she truly was but rather as the fulfillment of deep needs arising from his otherwise empty life. In this way, he had started at the culmination of love when he should have started at the beginning.

What should he have focused on in his first attempts at love? The humblest objects imaginable: "A tree. A rock. A cloud." When he learned to start from such simple beginnings, the man learned to love all things and all creatures.

A number of contemporary guides to living advise us to turn *inward*. They preach introspection — know thyself, heal thyself — as a directive for success in life and in love.

Yet, in our modern compartmentalized lives, many people already feel trapped in an isolation they did not choose. Many feel cut off from family roots by geographic distance. So, too, the jobs many of us do bring little sense of *connectedness* to other people.

This book has a fundamentally different message from these other guides to loving. It will urge you not merely to look inward but to turn *outward* — to seek fulfillment not just in an understanding of yourself but also in a genuine involvement with other people.

I had a great deal of help with this project. In addition to working with many patients over the years, I had the good fortune to meet thirty-two boys who live in three cottages in a place called Boys Haven, nestled on the flatlands of East Texas. The boys came from varied beginnings, but had one thing in common: nobody loved them. These young men have taught me far more than I could have learned in academic circles about love, and pain, and the possibility of real joy.

KMP

Part I

CHAPTER 1

Perspectives

Love is like many things in life; if we view it from different angles, the effect on us changes. When I think of how we might look at love from different perspectives, I think of a certain bay on the Gulf of Mexico where I've spent many hours sailing in a small boat. When the weather is good, the whole experience is beautiful. Surrounded by the calm and the blue and sunlight glistening on the water's surface, I feel solace and peace, protection and serenity. It's like the security of love: I feel that nothing can hurt or disturb me.

When the winds shift to the southeast, however, and a summer storm approaches, my feelings of peace are quickly shattered. As the sun is suddenly obscured by dark clouds and the calm blue water turns brown and rough, the gentle breeze that kept me so comfortable becomes a terrifying gale threatening my very survival. And, as in a love relationship, my impulse is to run away from the very things that gave me so much security and happiness minutes before.

One day, on a business trip, I flew over the bay in an airliner. Looking out the window from thirty thousand feet, I could see a panorama of the entire bay. From that height, the water looked neither protective nor threatening. It was as if someone had merely taken a glass of water and spilled it on a pavement. It looked almost unimportant. Seeing the bay from that perspective, I began to long for the good feelings of basking in the palm of Nature's hand again.

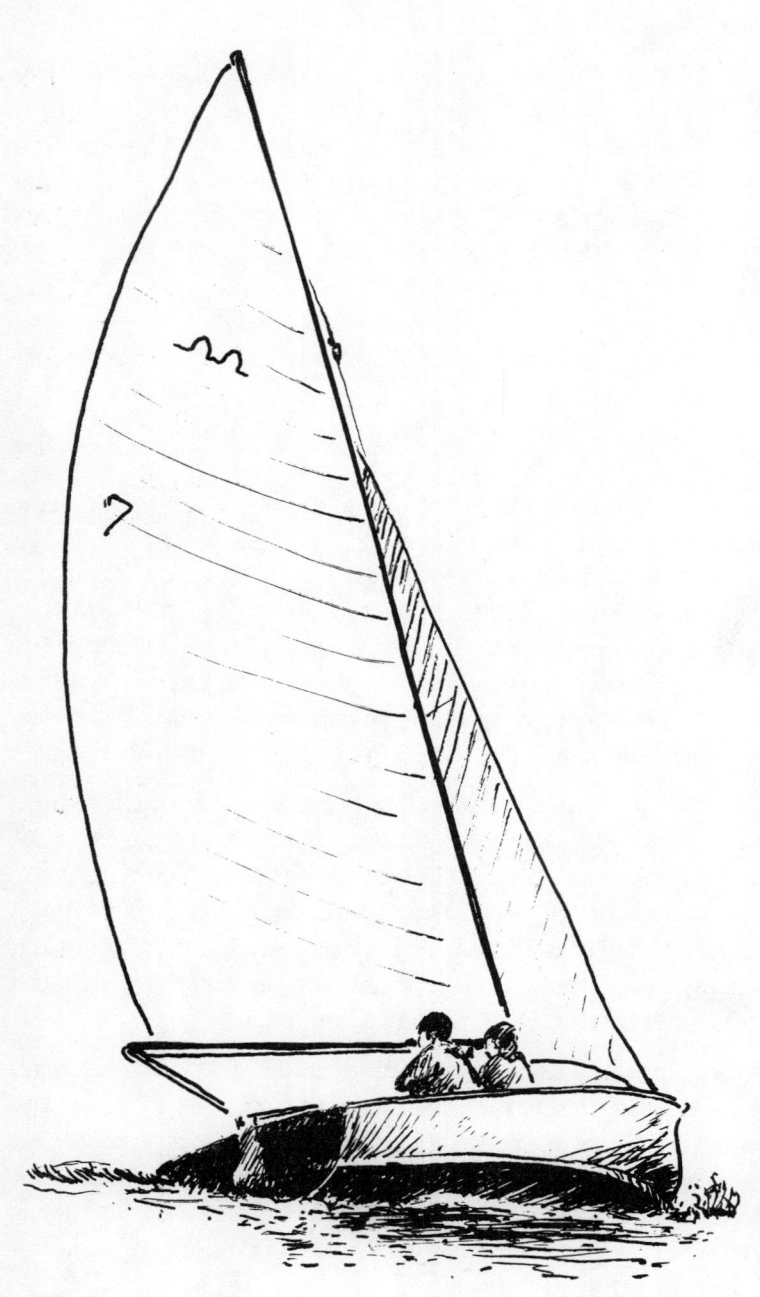

In visual perception, as in a love relationship, different perspectives produce different feelings. Sometimes it is good to be on the boat, enjoying the calm and the blue and the sun, warm and safe yet vulnerable to the storm; sometimes the storm makes us appreciate the peaceful times and helps us realize how strong we can be. But when love hurts, the secret to feeling good is to elevate our self-perspective, to rise to a higher level of living by adopting an attitude toward others in what I call practicing nurturing and caring behavior. From such a height, from such an elevated value on our own existence, we once again yearn for the calm and blue and peace of love.

It would be wonderful if we could change our vantage point on certain relationships at will. When the going was good, we would glide along and enjoy the ride; when the ride got rough, we would just fly above it all and look down and say, "From up here it looks like a big deal over nothing." Unfortunately, it is not that easy. If it were, none of us would go through the agony of indecision associated with quitting a job, severing a friendship, disowning a child, or getting a divorce.

Yet, the approach I am going to suggest when love hurts is far easier than trying to survive the emotional destruction often associated with severing a bond. I have hinted that the secret to flying above love's hurt is to elevate our view of ourselves by using nurturing and caring behavior as a therapy form. But being sensitive to and acting on the needs of the people around us is not enough. I know patients and therapists alike who immerse themselves in the needs of others (in counseling, in volunteer work, and in community action projects), but who suffer horribly in personal relationships.

They are on the right track, but the real benefit of their nurturing and caring loses its strength because they have not connected it to themselves sufficiently to elevate their own sense of self-worth. It's as if the medicine is being taken on schedule but is not getting to the diseased organ.

What is this connection, then, this link that relates your nurturing and caring to a higher perspective on your loving? It has two main

points: (1) The acts of nurturance must demonstrate your ability to cope effectively with situations and to sustain others in need. (2) They must not be isolated instances but must contribute to the development of new behavior patterns and habits of thought in you.

Consider, for example, a talented surgeon who brings life-saving skills to the operating room. Clearly this person has a power to help others that is almost godlike. Yet, if he or she performs operations mechanically and uncaringly, with little compassion for the person under the knife, then the surgeon is not likely to benefit very much from the deep fulfillment such nurturing might bring.

In your own case, you need not undertake years of training or possess highly specialized skills to nurture effectively enough to elevate your self-perspective. Think of a few of the possibilities open to you:

1. church groups
2. Girl and Boy Scout troops and Campfire Girls
3. Little League teams
4. nursing homes
5. community action committees
6. animal shelters
7. homes for the physically and emotionally handicapped and Special Olympics
8. orphanages
9. YMCA and YWCA
10. Big Brother organizations and Boys Clubs
11. hospices
12. prisons
13. women's shelters

A more comprehenisve list from which you can formulate your own plan of action to elevate your self-perspective above the pain of loving is in the

Appendix. Certainly, as you read on, you'll get a clear picture of what kinds of changes need to be made in your life plans. Right at home, unexpected small acts of caring may bring far-reaching results. Your nurturing need in fact may be no more complicated than listening attentively to a grandmother who delights in recounting stories of her youth in the old country. You can also make a special effort to give support to your parents, to be patient with your children and your children's friends, to tend to plants and animals, to be cheerful and friendly toward neighbors. These small acts are in no way extraordinary. Yet, sometimes all of us become so overburdened that we lose sight of the good we could be doing.

Nurturing and caring may of course take place at home, but there are special reasons why most people find it easier to develop new habits of thought and patterns of behavior outside the home. For one thing, relatives tend to take help for granted—or to forget to express their gratitude. Then, too, those you live with sometimes have firm, but limited, conceptions of what you are capable of doing. Moreover, many people get bogged down at home in routine tasks that leave little time and energy for projects of choice.

"Choice" is, in fact, a key word. A commitment to nurturing outside the home has the advantage of being chosen and clearly defined, both in time and in scope. You may choose to demonstrate your competence in a skill you already possess, or you may choose to develop a new one. You can be extremely daring or play it very safe. And every bit you do to help others counts in your quest of a new perspective on yourself.

The essential point is that in order to be happy in loving, it is essential to develop a good self-image, and you need to think of yourself as having a lot of value to the rest of the world.

People who are not happy with themselves are not desirable in any relationship. Bosses with an ego problem, wives who complain that nobody loves them, husbands who constantly prowl about looking for reinforcement of their maleness, children who take drugs, and friends

Perspectives 23

who chronically complain, are all people who make love hurt. Nurturing and caring behavior provides a strong framework, a firm sense of self-worth, so that you can rise above these relationships to a vantage point from which you can see them in perspective and alleviate the pain.

CHAPTER 2

Patterns

Ellen was the fourth unhappy person I saw that day. She was a married woman in her thirties with a mild weight problem, and she just couldn't stop eating.

I asked her how her marriage was, and she said blandly, "all right." Then: "It could be a whole lot better if we didn't bicker so much."

Last night, for instance, there had been a fight over potatoes. Yes, potatoes. She had wanted them fried, and he had wanted them boiled. He constantly reminded her how fattening fried food was, and the more he harped, the more she ate fattening foods. She said she really didn't want to be fat, but when Henry started nagging and criticizing her weight, it was like being overcome by some mysterious demon.

Like everyone else, she was feeling bad today. The senseless fighting had taken its toll on her mood.

I asked her if she understood why this was going on. She said his nagging was like a switch that seemed to turn on her eating motor. I hated to ask the question about her parents, but I knew one of them must have given her a hard time about her eating habits.

It turned out to be her mother. She had wanted Ellen to be a fashion model, and had constantly badgered her about her weight. All that criticism had given Ellen one big message: no matter what she did, Ellen wasn't quite acceptable. It didn't matter that the reproof had been spoken for Ellen's own good, nor did it matter that it had been said out of love. It had nevertheless been received and translated as a message of unacceptability, and every time Henry said something about her weight, Ellen heard a reinforcement of that message.

Over the years, she had heard this message so often that she had begun to believe it herself. People who believe they're unacceptable start to act unacceptable, and Ellen soon gave up caring how she looked. She knew her mother hadn't meant it, but the message had seemed so clear: "You would make me much happier if you were thin." To the child inside Ellen, there had to be some retribution for this terrible hurt, and there was no more perfect vengeance than getting fat— something fashion models didn't do.

Her mother had unknowingly damned her to a life of vengeance, of eating too much and grooming too little every time a critical, non-accepting word was said to her by *anybody*. Her mother had set her on this course, and her relationships with other people had all followed this destructive parallel. In each case there had been a triggering episode, perhaps only a word, that reminded Ellen that she wasn't quite okay. If the supper burned, or a plant died, or even if someone else had a problem, the setback somehow echoed that message of unacceptability, and the hurt and vengeance started again: the mysterious demon would overcome her and Ellen would start eating uncontrollably.

Henry was good at keeping Ellen on this parallel track. It was important for him to have a pretty wife, and the fatter Ellen got, the less interested in sex Henry got. The less he touched Ellen, the more unacceptable she felt, and the more she felt this way, the more she ate.

So the argument over the potatoes was only the tip of the iceberg. At the root of their bickering was this reiterated message of unacceptability, first transmitted early in Ellen's life, then unknowingly reinforced over and over again.

It was a wonderful insight, but Ellen had heard it before. She had been to two psychologists, a psychiatrist, and a marriage counselor before her visits to me.

"I know I have some hangups, but doesn't everybody? I just want to lose some weight. There's no way to change the past . . . I certainly can't change my husband, and I don't have the money for a divorce."

△ ▽ △

She was absolutely right. It wouldn't help a bit to get another husband, because, given her predilections, she would probably choose someone just like her first. And really, her husband's demands were not unreasonable. Besides, even if she did find the perfect, non-critical, totally accepting husband, she would still be vulnerable to the criticisms of others around her. Everything that went wrong in daily living would remind her of that repeated message of unacceptability and send her on a rampage of vengeance eating. Apparently the imprinting by her mother had been so powerful that Ellen now repeatedly found herself on a charted course of pain and humiliation.

Clearly Ellen needed to change. She needed to understand her old tendencies and start on a new course with more flattering and supportive ideas about herself. Though still surrounded by the same people, she could then establish new parallels that would make her feel good about herself.

△ ▽ △

I thought about Ellen later that day and realized that she had been one of many who had had some kind of problem with

other people, and not just spouses, either. The first patient had had a problem with his son, the second had had a dispute with a boss, and the third and fourth had been dealing with marital problems. I asked myself "When love hurts, are we to retreat to an island where no pain (in the form of human interaction) can touch us?" Often in the throes of love we try to do just that. Yet when we find ourselves alone, we panic and quickly find someone to talk to, thus opening ourselves once more to the possiblity of hurt.

△   ▽   △

All of us have found ourselves in love and in pain. Oddly, the relationships that don't really hurt us don't seem to excite us much either. Our most intense friendships seem to draw us into them—we tend to prefer friends with whom we can share higher highs and lower lows. Similarly, we find ourselves in overpowering love affairs that consume us and tear us apart yet, in some mysterious way, hold us tenaciously. The intensity of these relationships gives us a euphoric strength to face each day, and by the same token, the slightest word or gesture taken the wrong way incapacitates us.

It is the pain associated with this intense type of relationship that often drives us to seek help. We want a divorce, but multitudes of reasons, some valid, some ridiculous, keep us from severing the bond. We want to quit our job, deal with our children differently, or avoid certain friends, yet the same mysterious barrier to action stands in our way. And many times we wangle our way out of one painful situation, only to find ourselves in a parallel situation with a different person. It's as if the plot of the play is the same over and over, but the actors and actresses change with each season.

Every therapist looks for such patterns from the past, whether the therapist tells patients so or not. For these submerged parallels do, indeed, resurface in later years. Yet, as we shall see, it is also possible to stop the play and rewrite the script.

CHAPTER 3

Changing

During my psychiatry residency, I had a special fondness for a patient named Ronnie who was, as the staff demeaningly labeled him, an "organic." The less-than-flattering term "organic" was given to patients with Organic Brain Syndrome—a disease in which some of the higher coordinating centers of the brain are short-circuited. Ronnie was a brute of a figure. He was five foot ten, broad at the shoulders, and must have weighed two-fifty.

He was not a favorite of the hospital staff, probably because he wasn't an "interesting" case, the kind so often sought after by admitting psychiatrists. Ronnie simply acted the way he was treated, and treated others the way they acted around him. There was no dilution of this simple stimulus-response reaction, as normally occurs from other brain input such as ideas of right-and-wrong, emotion, or logical thought process. A simple gift of a candy bar would have Ronnie camping outside an office door in adoring fealty, while a heartfelt slap on the back might produce an outburst of violent, assaultive "retaliation." It was no accident that Ronnie's eyeglasses were held together in four places by adhesive tape.

The most memorable instance of Ronnie's absolute eye-for-an-eye attitude took place in an elevator. The hospital was visited one day by none other than the State Commissioner of Health, kind of a *capo di tutti capo* of bureaucrats. He was such a condescending fellow that nobody liked him. He called everyone "young man" or "young lady" regardless of age or position in the hospital, and he never looked anyone straight in the eye. Like a true politician, the Commissioner offered well-placed smiles and handshakes, occasionally slapping a few backs and giving a few hugs.

He met his match when he stepped into an elevator with Ronnie. We never found out exactly what happened, but with the addition of a few pieces of adhesive tape, the Commissioner's eyeglasses were almost as good as new.

The extremely valuable lesson in all this was that I could get Ronnie to do anything I wanted simply by behaving differently in front of him. In all my years in psychiatry after that, I would be reminded of Ronnie whenever a patient expressed hopelessness about love, saying: "He or she will never change." As human beings, we all possess the power to change behavior toward others, much as Ronnie could, though in general less quickly and (one hopes) less graphically.

If you don't like the way you're being treated in a relationship, then you should act differently. The man who acts like a tyrant in his marriage gets treated like a tyrant by his wife and kids, with all the necessary lip-service, sneaking around, and truth-padding. The woman who acts like a doormat in such a relationship gets treated exactly like one.

Many times, as you well know, acting differently in a relationship is more easily said than done. For one thing, you may be reluctant, or even embarrassed, to play a new role, or write a new script—in fact, to shake the complacent expectations of those who know you best. If for a time you could move exclusively among strangers—people who have no firm expectations against which to measure your behavior— you might be able to act out a new part without fear of failure or humiliation.

Fear itself prevents people from acting differently in many situations, but in love relationships, it can be especially immobilizing. There is, however, a way to neutralize this fear, and that is to change the way you perceive yourself within the relationship. How you see yourself in a love relationship is what reaches the emotion centers of your brain and gives you either the courage that permits action or the fear that inhibits it. With the exception of the real physical fear associated with spouse or child abuse, fear in relationships is almost always based on subjective perception, and not on objective truth.

If it's pitch-black in the house and you are lying in bed trying to go to sleep, a whirring noise followed by a crunching sound ending with "whhooommph" will certainly get your attention. You might suspect that an alien robot has whirred up to your back door, forced it open with a powerful pincer-like arm, and then knocked into something on the way down the hall to the bedroom to do to you whatever terrible things alien robots do. In the daytime, when light and noise are present to distract the senses and thus reassure the emotional centers of hte brain, you can remain unafraid long enough to make a rational judgement about the noises. It is not an alien robot, but only your refrigerator's very un-alien icemaker.

I am reminded of a patient named Barbara who demonstrated this idea of fear and perception very well. She never came to me for therapy, but was a medical patient whom I saw only periodically for a cold or a sore throat. Barbara was an extremely pleasant whoman who never tried to get the upper hand in own small talk; I surmised that this was a reflection of her relationship with her husband.

Only once did she mention a problem in her marriage: it was that whe hated to ask her husband for money. It was such a demeaning thing, and it made her feel like a child.

When Barbara suggested to her husband that they have equal power over the checking account, he would always refuse and discourage further discussion by pouting for a few days. He did give her an allowance, but such things are given to kids, not spouses, and the allowance only reinforced her *perception* of herself as a child looking to her benevolent husband/father for sustenance. She didn't think a job would help, because she could

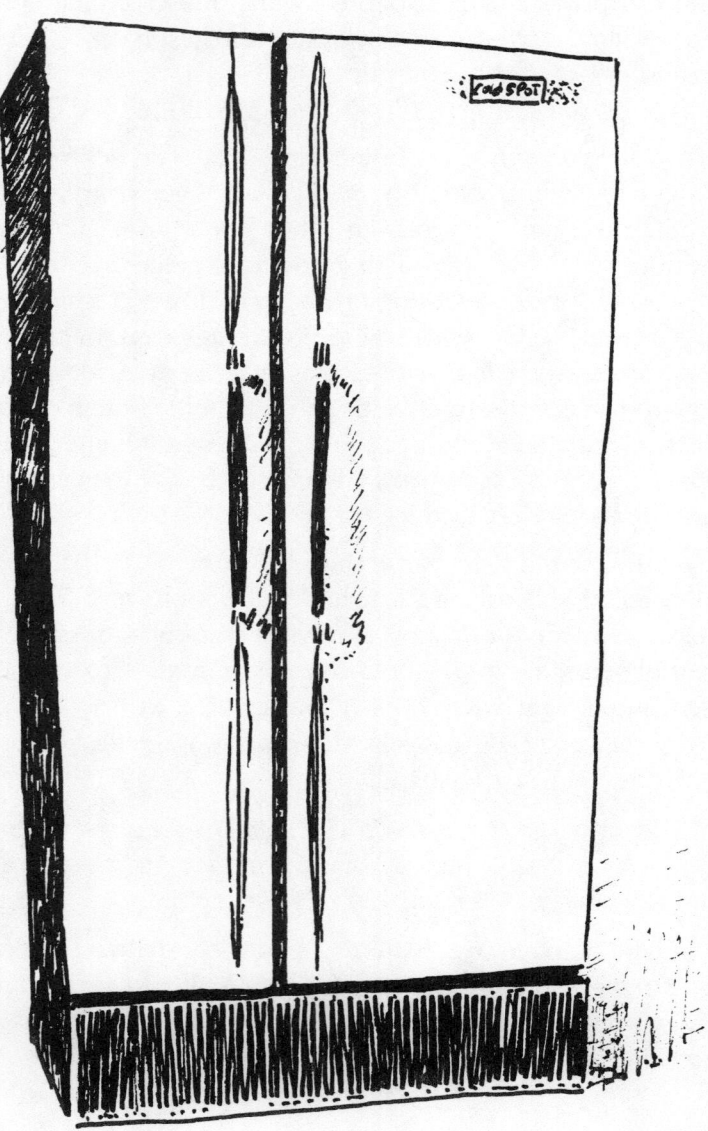

work only part-time, since she had children and a home to take care of Besides, why should she hold down two jobs—part time employment as well as the household duties—while her husband had only one job?

What Barbara needed was to change her preception of herself in the relationship from one of having *no* power to one of having *some* power. Her husband, for whatever reasons of immaturity, did not see her housework as contributing to the family's well-being; he saw only money as achieving that end. Money was his basis for having a say in the marriage, a view facetiously referred to by counselors as the "Golden Rule": "them's that's got the gold makes the rules."

Since money had such clout in the relationship, I asked Barbara if getting a job would help to demonstrate her "worth." To compensate her for the time she spent working at thome doing household chores, I suggested that she ask her husband to match her salary dollar for dollar. There would be no more begging for money; he would simply write a check based on her outside job's hourly pay rate. More important than the extra money would be Barbara's perception of herself as having greater worth in the relationship, as being a money-earning, card-carrying adult.

She thought for a second and said that she'd already considered the idea. Her husband, however, didn't really want her to work.

"A double-edged sword," I said. "Your husband doesn't want you to have money of your own either way."

I told her the problem wasn't really with money, it was with power and her husband's perception of it. He wasn't so unsure of Barbara's ability to handle money as he was of his own ability to provide for the family. He felt if he were in the driver's seat, he could more effectively control the family's welfare. Barbara's working and having money wasn't so much a threat to him; it just got in the way of his controlling things.

She had no choice. To solve her dilemma, she *had* to walk one of the sharp edges of the sword, and she wisely chose to get a part-time job. While her husband at first expressed his displeasure, he soon saw her persistence at earning extra money as a supportive measure in their marriage.

His perception of his wife changed from seeing her as a dependent to seeing her as a supporter, and yet his perception of his own power escaped unchanged. Barbara, in reality, had usurped some of that power, and yet maintained peaceful balance in the marriage by bringing about change purely in how she saw herself.

△ ▽ △

Not all solutions can be as neat as this, however. Many troubles throughout life hinge on relationships, not only with lovers, but with boses, children, and friends. Since severing these relationships is often impractical and sometimes very painful, you need to elevate your perception of your whole life to a higher plane, so that you can see yourself as having a greater worth to the world. If you have a higher opinion of your value to the world, you will act with greater assurance and be treated in relationships on a level more suited to your needs.

In order to elevate your perception of your worth to the world, you need to consider nurturing and caring behavior as therapeutic. If you develop an attitude of nurturing and caring for others, you can put an end to your own isolation and develop a bond with your fellow creatures who may be in need. This bond gives you a self-perception of power, and with this power you will begin to gain confidence in your own competency and effectiveness. From this improved vantage point, you will quite naturally begin to expect (and even demand) a greater fulfillment in your life.

This would be, in essence, the beginning of the end of love's hurting you.

CHAPTER 4

A Framework For Loving

Whenever we look at finished products (ourselves, our love relationships) and try to identify the ingredients that went into their make-up, we are dabbling in the science of analytics. To say that I am about to "dabble" in analytical psychology is a dangerous statement indeed. Since Freud, psychological writing has reflected vigorous controversy about the human personality, and for me to suggest dabbling in it is as impudent as proposing to write a ten-page pamphlet on nuclear physics. So let me tread softly, and let us understand among ourselves that I am asking from the hallowed science of analytical psychology only the bits and pieces that will immediately serve our understanding of why we love and why loving is painful.

△ ▽ △

My humility derives from my training. During my residency at the old Buffalo State Hospital, there was a professor named Cedric Lasker who was also a graduate of a leading school of psychoanalysis. He always wore a black homburg and a black suit and drove a black Cadillac. *Every* lecture he started with, "Good morning, ladies and gentlemen. My name is Cedric Lasker. I am a psychoanalyst, and you are not." Since that time, I have been very wary of the color black, and even more careful about delving into people's past.

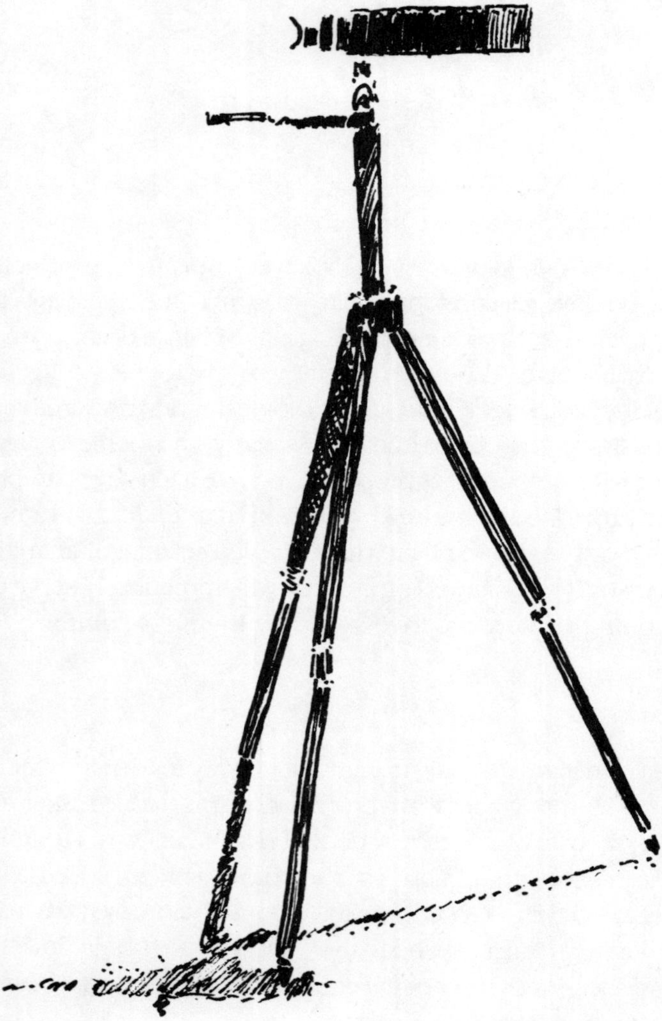

Yet, insight gained from looking back may be helpful for several reasons. First, understanding why something is hurting us can itself alleviate some of the pain, even though insight doesn't always lead to constructive action. Employees are likely to be more tolerant of a boss's ranting and ravings if they are aware that a fatal tumor is growing in his head. No constructive action can be taken in such a case, but simple insight eases some of the tensions associated with the boss's behavior. So, too, with loving and relating to others: if you have some understanding of why you feel and act the way you do, then the hurt you suffer becomes more of a price paid than a punishment meted out.

Second, and more important, if you discover where you have weak spots in the framework of your being and loving, this knowledge, in turn, will help you avoid putting stress on sensitive areas of your personality.

For example, a man who unknowingly harbors anger toward his mother because she was ill and a little short on nurturing when he was a child will be vulnerable in his emotional attraction to strong, feisty, controlling women who project an image of mothering and nurturing. The trouble usually starts when these capable, ambitious women seek jobs to fulfill their personal needs, then unfortunately begin to replay the less-than-attentive role associated with "mother." Insight into such a weak spot might alleviate the immediate furor, even though it may not fully dissipate the entrenched anger the man feels toward his mother.

In order to gain helpful insight, I am going to spend the next several chapters looking at three ways our framework for loving is shaped (or mis-shaped) and how these three "support beams" are held together at the apex to form a pyramid of sorts. This make-believe pyramid forms the base which supports all our love relationships. Other relationships (including friendships, work associations, and love for pets and children) are like cross-spars which usually, although not always, support and strengthen the pyramid.

What are these three "support beams" that determine not only how strong and solid your love relationships will be, but also who will balance, with proper stability, atop the pyramid?

The first supporting leg is what I call "the Survival Plan." It is your own image of yourself as being able to make it through life and your strategy for doing so. It is not perfectly synonymous with your self-image, which includes many additional goals, anxieties, and attributes, but is an important part of it. Although based on an inborn survival instinct, the Survival Plan is also cultured and shaped by parents and others around you. If you develop a secure Survival Plan during childhood, then this supporting beam will be a strong one, providing a stable foundation for loving. If, however, you left childhood unsure of your ability to survive, then your love relationships will probably suffer because you will expend too much energy in non-constructive forms of ego-reinforcement (demanding dependency from your lover, side relationships for emotional support, high-risk business ventures, seeking unrealistic fortunes, and so on.)

If the first support beam of the love pyramid is your view of yourself as a surviving and functioning individual, the second is your opinion of the objects of your loving: the opposite sex if you are heterosexual and the same sex if you are homosexual.* Obviously, you form very strong opinions about the opposite sex from your parent of that same sex, and, as we shall see later, this very influential teacher may have left you with some rather mixed impressions. All these impressions are part of what I call "the Love Debt." This is an often not-so-pleasant legacy of injustice, based on a perceived predator-victim relationship between parents, that the child is left to "pay off" or "make right" later in life.

The third leg of the imaginary pyramid is again a collection of experiences, not about how you see yourself or others, but about what you expect from love. This is what I call "the Romantic Ideal": a vast storehouse of notions and images of what love should be that you have garnered throughout life from parents, friends, lovers, books, television programs, songs and movies. Holding excessively romantic expectations of loving leads to fairy-tale visions in close relationships and often places impossible demands on the other person. Yet, a Romantic Ideal is impor-

---

*Although I am limiting this discussion to heterosexual relationships, much of the theory holds true for homosexual relationships as well. Readers may wish to transpose aspects of the theory to accommodate them to personal lifestyles.

The Love Pyramid

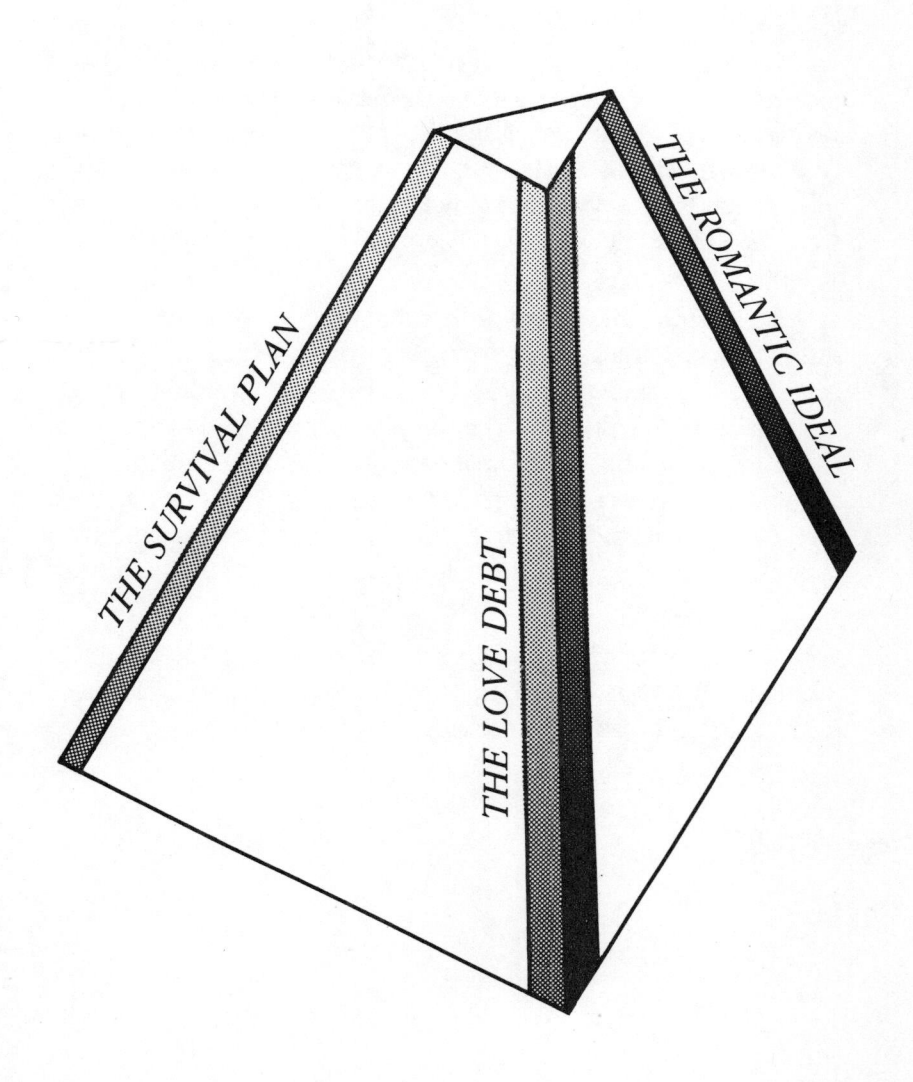

THE SURVIVAL PLAN

THE LOVE DEBT

THE ROMANTIC IDEAL

tant. Paradoxically, it is the mystery of romance that keeps many relationships from stagnating.

Can the three bases of loving ever change? Yes, they can and do. Throughout your life, multitudes of influences, some good and some bad, affect your self-image and the opinions you have of the opposite sex. Your romantic ideals are not only constantly changed by what you see around you, but go through timed-cycles of their own depending on your age and station in life.

You'll see later that as you go through life, you mold and shape your perceptions of lovers as if to cast them in a kind of play. The plot of this play moves toward the fulfillment of needs and wants based on the three support beams of the Love Pyramid: what you need and want for your own survival and well-being; what you need and want to right the "wrongs" inflicted by one parent-figure upon the other; and what you hope to get out of loving.

To illustrate these ideas further, I might present dozens of case studies. But such things really belong in medical journals. Instead, I am going to tell at some length a story of four people. It is a true story of life in a small town in East Texas. The characters are very real—they are, in fact, friends, neighbors, and patients of mine, with enough story-alteration to protect their privacy. But the fact-juggling has been minimal and really unimportant. Indeed, the dynamics that motivate these people are so universal, more than a few of my friends and patients will be convinced the stories are theirs.

Perhaps you will see something of yourself in the figures of Elizabeth, John, Mark and Walter. I hope so, and I hope you will benefit from hearing the story of their pain and their healing.

Part II

CHAPTER 5

Newcomers

I had been sailing the day they moved in, so when I got home I saw only a glimpse of their belongings being carried up the front walk from the orange van. Watching people move in is like catching them naked: the customary order and veneer are stripped away, and the innards of their lives exposed for all to see. What little I saw told me these were people who lived well, or tried to, but were perhaps stretching a bit.

As the last pieces were carried in, I thought to myself: whoever they were, they are now part of the little world of Sugar Creek.

The name Sugar Creek probably has belonged to a thousand such places. We didn't even have a creek, just rows of expensive look-alike houses, some a little bigger than others. Some of the houses were so similar inside that there was a standing neighborhood joke: the burglars on some streets didn't even need a flashlight to find the bathroom.

The newcomers' house was a smaller one, well-styled, four doors down from me, on the arc of the cul-de-sac. I found out from the neighborhood grapevine that he was an insurance salesman in his forties, she was a realtor in her late thirties, and they had a daughter away at school living with her boyfriend. There were whispers that they had lost a son to leukemia ten years or so ago.

I didn't actually see them until two days later. The Cadillac lumbered by me as I was picking up the morning paper, and she waved. I waved back and watched her eyes follow mine as she passed. She was a

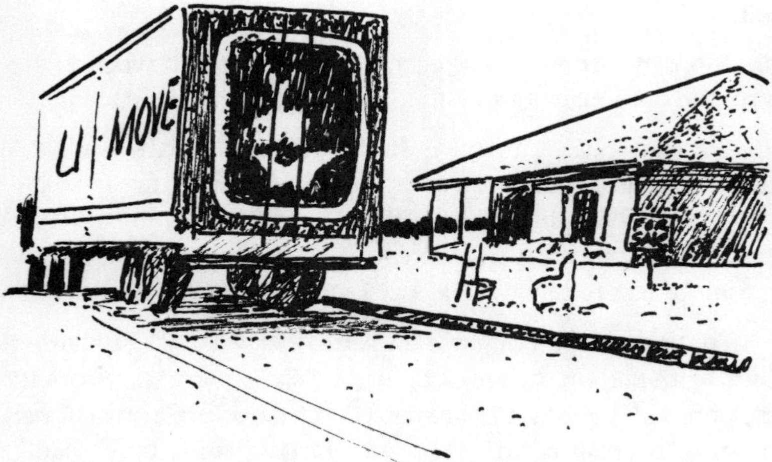
U-MOVE

pretty woman, dressed and made up carefully, and she had enough air of interest about her to make me want to talk with her sometime.

That evening I got the chance. Taking Beauregard for his nightly ritual walk, I stopped to chat.

Her name was Elizabeth. She was unloading groceries from her trunk, and seemed eager to talk, as if she already knew me. She smiled.

"This is a lucky break. I just moved in and a shrink walks up to my door."

I pointed to the bassett hound at my feet and said,

"You talking to me or him?"

She laughed and introduced herself, and then her husband, Mark, who was coming out for another armful of groceries to carry in. I wondered how she knew who I was, but she was a realtor, and such people make it their business to know the neighborhood.

They made a handsome, appropriate couple, but it was clear that she wanted to be friendlier than he. He listened to only a few words of the small talk exchanged, and then grabbed two more bags to carry in.

I took them in more closely. Neither was especially tall, and both were grappling with thirty extra pounds. With Mark's bearded and mustached face, the extra weight gave him a boyish look. It had a different effect on Elizabeth. Seen close up, she looked a bit more matronly than I had expected.

As the small talk ran out, I felt uncomfortable standing there alone with Elizabeth, and bade the appropriate "we-must-get-together" good-byes. We did not, however, get together. I don't know if it was the pressures of moving or her husband's fears of outsiders, but I didn't see them again for few weeks.

There was an end-of-the-summer party at the Willis', and the neighbors were already celebrating when I arrived. Mark was mixing well with everyone, seemingly skilled at superficial min-

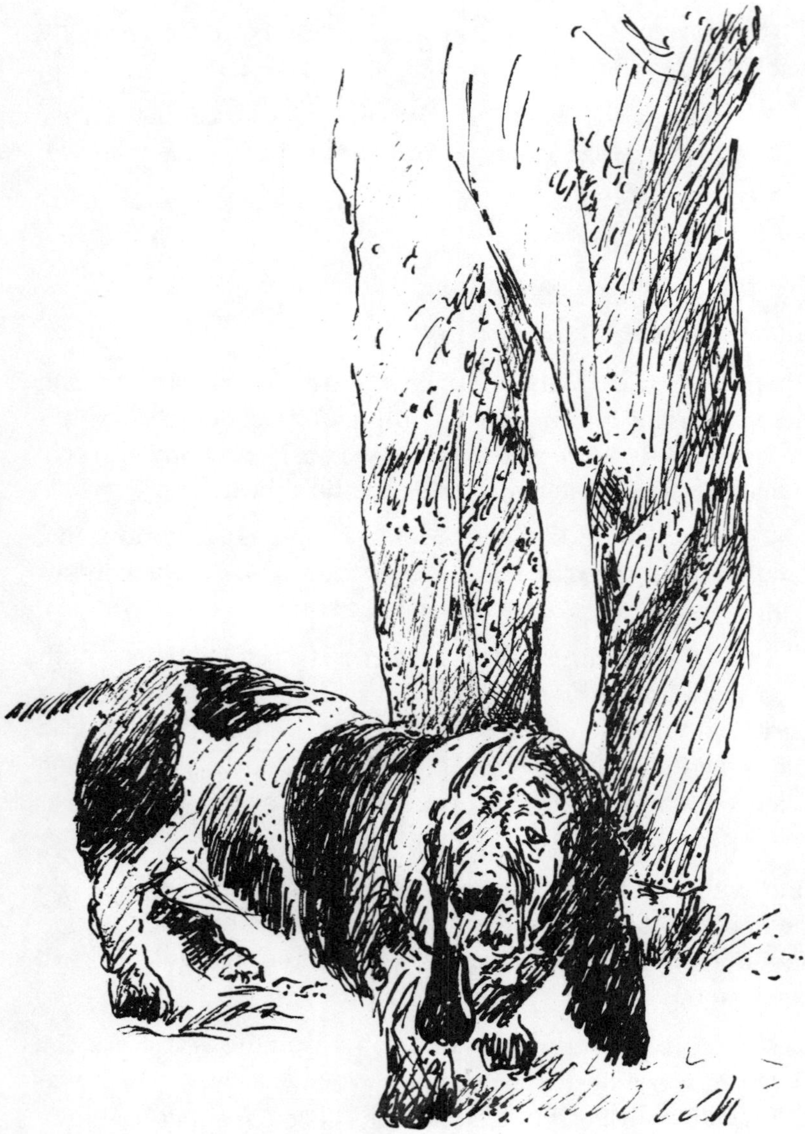

gling, but Elizabeth had cornered Ed Willis and was talking a blue streak about something unpleasant.

I greeted a few neighbors and wound up in a trio listening to Mark talk. He had our attention even though we'd heard similar pitches before.

"There is not one single person in this neighborhood who should have to pay a dime in Federal income taxes, ever. With the shelters we have available right now . . . "

Ye gods, he was a tax-scam peddler who made his money off the angry people stuck in the 50 percent bracket. I waited and listened through the cattle deals, the oil wells, and the real estate shuffling. He was sincere in his feelings, but obviously a man severely concerned with image and money.

I felt sorry for him. He was a semi-successful pettifogger talking a pitch to men who had been burned two or three times before. Mark sensed that, I think, and his fears of losing the crowd were being washed down with too much scotch.

Elizabeth meanwhile must have been telling Ed Willis some things that he thought he shouldn't be hearing because he seemed relieved to get away from her grasp. By the time I got to say hello, her eyes were red from the gin, and she looked tired. I wondered if she had been talking about her marriage.

I had seen the incidents replayed at other parties: a man or woman who seems to possess more than most people corners some captive listener in the kitchen and, as the alcohol flows, talks non-stop about the intimate details of an unhappy relationship. I was sure Ed Willis had already heard an earful.

I was cautious and I kept a neutral ground with Elizabeth.

"How do you like the neighborhood so far?"

She looked away. "The neighborhood's fine. My life is rotten."

Those were strong words to tell a virtual stranger, but I was being baited. She knew my business, and was trying to see if I wanted to help her; she assumed that talking to me would be different from talking to Ed Willis. She knew for a fact that we wouldn't talk in the kitchen of some neighborhood bash, and that talking to me professionally would cost a fair amount of money.

"Things gone downhill since you moved in?"

"Nothing new. Business is lousy. Mark's drinking too much again, and I'm getting fat as a pig. Of course, Mark drinks when I lose weight, too. . . . I wish I could afford you."

I was very careful with words to answer that.

"Money's a problem for you, huh?" It was an observation more than a question looking for an answer. She wasn't exactly telling me she expected a discount or free service, but she was saying that therapy probably wouldn't solve her problems, and that the money would be wasted.

I steered the conversation into a lighter vein, and she didn't seem to object. She apparently was quite an accomplished pianist who used to be a teacher before her venture into real estate. I listened for a while about her love of music, and then I said,

"I've always liked the piano. Maybe we could swap services."

She brightened at the idea. She pulled at my hand as if to examine it, and said:

"Marvelous hands. You'll make a good student."

I set my drink down and slowly retracted my hand; I put it in my pocket and turned to leave.

"I'm not the pupil. The lessons are for someone else. Call me Monday at my office."

CHAPTER 6

The Actors

Elizabeth never called me that Monday; apparently her feelings returned to normal when the alcohol wore off. What with all their problems, she and Mark must have felt they didn't fit into the neighborhood, but in fact they did. They had much the same grief we all had; they were just more melodramatic about it.

Later that week, I went to see the boy I had hoped would get some "free" piano lessons from Elizabeth. He was an eleven-year-old named John—not Jack, Johnny, or any other nickname, just John. He lived at Boys Haven, and I had met him a few months before.

Boys Haven is a charity home in Sugar Creek. I guess most towns have such places—"homes" for boys who are homeless or who are the victims of abusive parents or step-parents. When foster homes aren't available for these kids, it gives them somewhere to go. Thirty-two boys currently lived at Boys Haven. One of them, John, sorely needed a friend, and the Administrator had asked me to look out for him.

John was one of those remnants of society's mistakes that none of us likes to think about. his mother had left when he was seven. No one had any idea where she went; she had just vanished. A younger sister had been taken in by an aunt and uncle, and John had been left with his father: a seven-year-old innocent entrusted to the care of a hopeless and violent alcoholic. Before his eighth birthday, John had been placed in Boys Haven, cigarette burns and all.

And he had been there ever since, doing his best in school, behaving

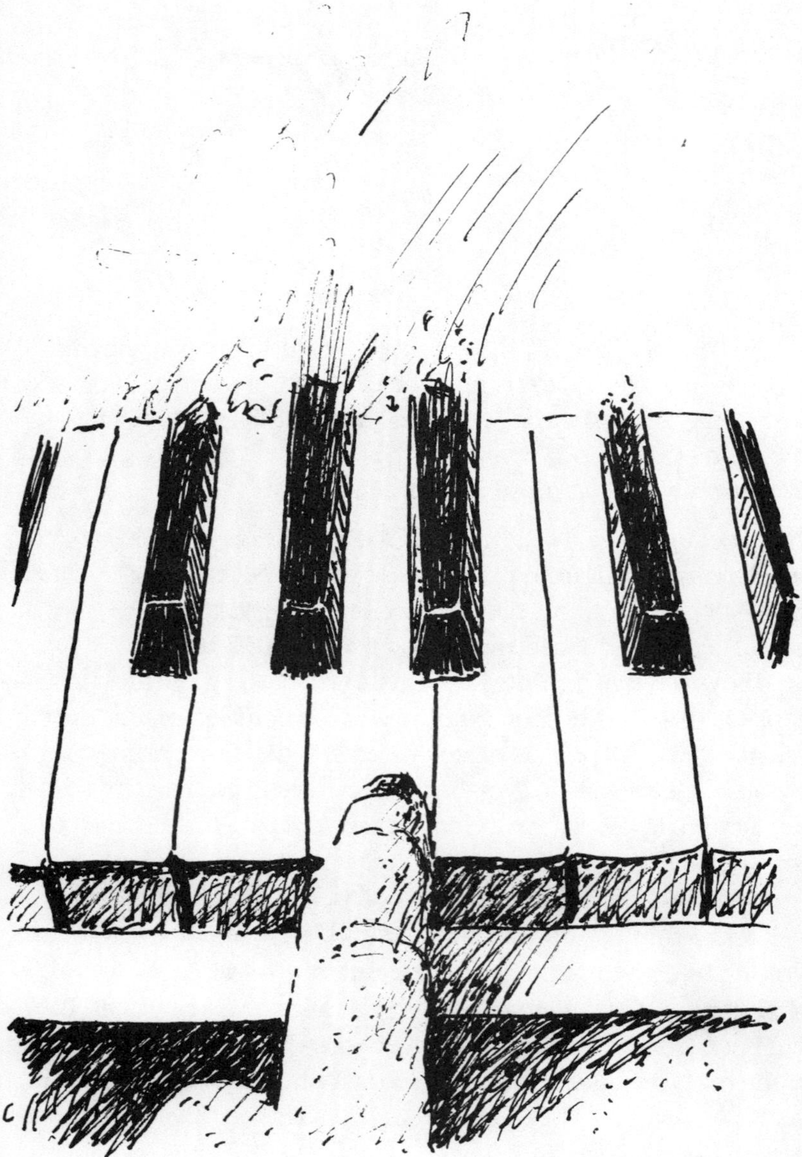

The Actors 53

as well as he could, and generally looking for love and acceptance from the world.

I had befriended him with small gifts and laughter, and during this little visit, I had planned to broach the subject of piano lessons.

When I arrived, he was dressed as if he were on his way to church: clean trousers and shirt (both too big) and hair ostentatiously slicked down. I knew the fuss wasn't for me because he hadn't known I was coming, but it had to be for something important: eleven-year-olds don't normally clean up like that in the middle of the week.

I soon found out he was dressed up because his father was coming to pick him up. As he talked with me, he kept nervously watching for the car to drive up. His father had promised him they'd eat supper out, and then go shopping. The house-parents told me the same script was replayed every three months or so, and the fellow usually didn't even show up. Yet John's loyalty was unwavering.

I wondered about this man, this actor in the script, who had such an undeserved loyalty from John. He was, really, the only thing left in John's survival plan. I don't suppose any of the boys at the Haven saw their early life much differently. As abused and abandoned as the boys were, the family remnants —alcoholic parents and inadequate stepparents—were all they had to bolster up their plans for making it through life.

A rusted '74 Pinto drove up. The mystery man—an unshaven and unkempt alcoholic—was driving. John's face lit up in renewed hope, and he ran out the door and jumped into the battered car as if it were a white horse conveying a shining knight.

My own hopes for a different ending were bouyed also by this appearance. After all, people do change, and the old man did show up this time.

I made small talk with the house-parents, said my good-byes, and was walking out of the dormitory when I saw them again. Barely five minutes had passed, and John and his father were back from their "all-day" excursion. Their "dinner and shopping" had turned out to be a

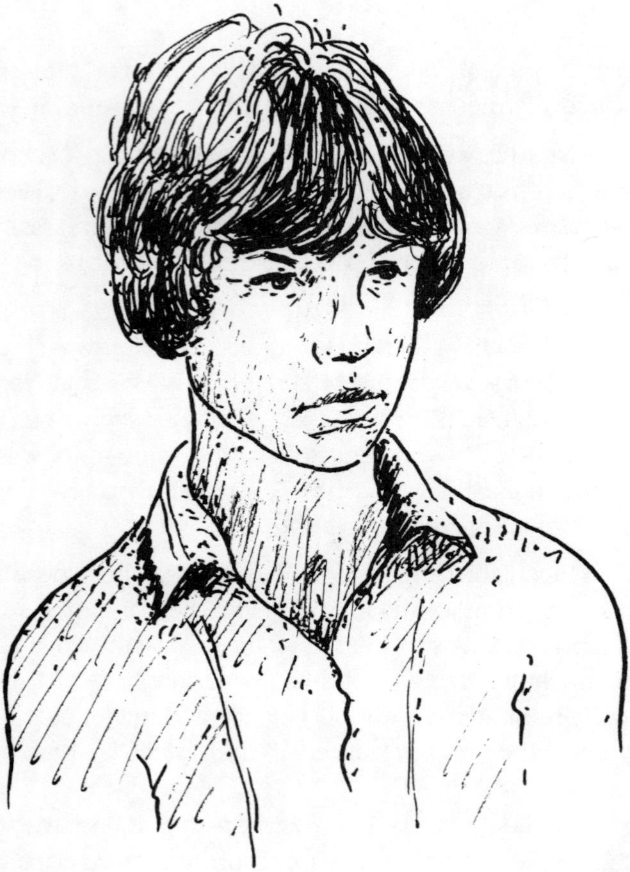

five-minute trip to the Stop-N-Go for a Pepsi.

John got out of the car without speaking, clutching that bottle of cola as if it were gold, and watched his knight-on-the-white-horse drive off. For the longest time, he stood there at the curb and stared until the Pinto was out of sight. His expression was flat; he showed neither smile nor tear. He looked like a lost angel left on a cloud with no reference points to anything in his life.

He walked by me and said only that his Dad had to work and would be back another day. He had gone inside when I realized that, for the first time in a long while, I had tears in my eyes.

And the angels sang:

Hush, little baby, don't say a word,
Daddy's gonna buy you a mockingbird.
If that mockingbird won't sing,
Daddy's gonna buy you a diamond ring.
If that diamond ring turns brass,
Daddy's gonna buy you a looking glass.
If that looking glass gets broke,
Daddy's gonna buy you an ox with yoke.

If that ox with yoke won't pull,
Daddy's gonna buy you a cart and bull.
If that bull and cart fall down,
You'll still be the sweetest babe in town.

△   ▽   △

Bad marriages go through cycles of storm and peace, just like good marriages, but bad ones have longer storms that are often very close together. Less than two weeks after the Willis' party, the next storm hit Elizabeth and Mark. I got an emergency phone call from the answering service. It was Elizabeth.

"I need to talk to you. "I . . . I'm going to get a divorce, and I don't know if I can handle it."

I told her I preferred not to talk about it over the phone, and that, if the piano lesson swap was okay, I would see her the next day. I was well aware of her ambivalence about the matter of therapy, and making her sleep on it would be a fair test of how serious she was. I thought there was a good chance that her feelings would dissipate as they had after the Willis' party, and before a commitment to therapy *and* to John's piano lessons was made, I felt Elizabeth should be fully ready to get off the see-saw she was living on.

I was right in making Elizabeth wait for an appointment. Her see-saw feelings continued to tear her up; she not only failed to make the appointment for the next day but actually repeated this pattern three more times over the next two-and-a-half months. She became more embarrassed each time she called, but I reassured her this was precisely why I included the 24-hour waiting period-escape mechanism. The holidays were coming, and I was sure the frequency of her troubles would increase—along with the severity.

This time Mark called. Elizabeth had told him she had taken some pills, but wouldn't say how many. I told Mark I would wait in my office until she was checked out in an emergency room, and asked him to call me to set up a time that same day.

No one called; I assumed the little drama had driven them into a fit of passionate forgiveness and resolve. Indeed, Elizabeth's flair for histrionics was her only weapon against Mark.

The next time there was a storm, Elizabeth decided the see-saw was too much. She showed up.

△   ▽   △

I watched her walk in from the car to the office. She was dressed stylishly as usual, but in subdued tones; her walk confirmed her mixed feelings about therapy. There was definitely part of her that didn't want this baring of the soul, and she came forward slowly, her shoulders stooped.

When it was time, I showed her into my office after a very informal greeting.

"How ya' doin', kiddo? C'mon in and sit down."

She was clearly very nervous and immediately noticed an old black leather reclining couch in the corner.

"Oh God, do I have to lay on the couch? . . . or is it 'lie' on the couch?"

"Depends what you wanna do on the couch. It's good for afternoon naps, but since we're going to talk today, I think these chairs'll do fine." She seemed glad I was saying something; it made her relax a bit.

We sat opposite each other for a second or two and settled into our chairs. She was wearing a pair of those new stylish tinted glasses that make people look stellar, and I asked her to take them off.

"I need to see your eyes; they say a lot about your feelings."

"I feel funny without my glasses."

"Do you need them to see?"

"No, just reading, and shading my eyes . . . "

I butted in, " . . . and hiding."

The therapeutic process had begun.

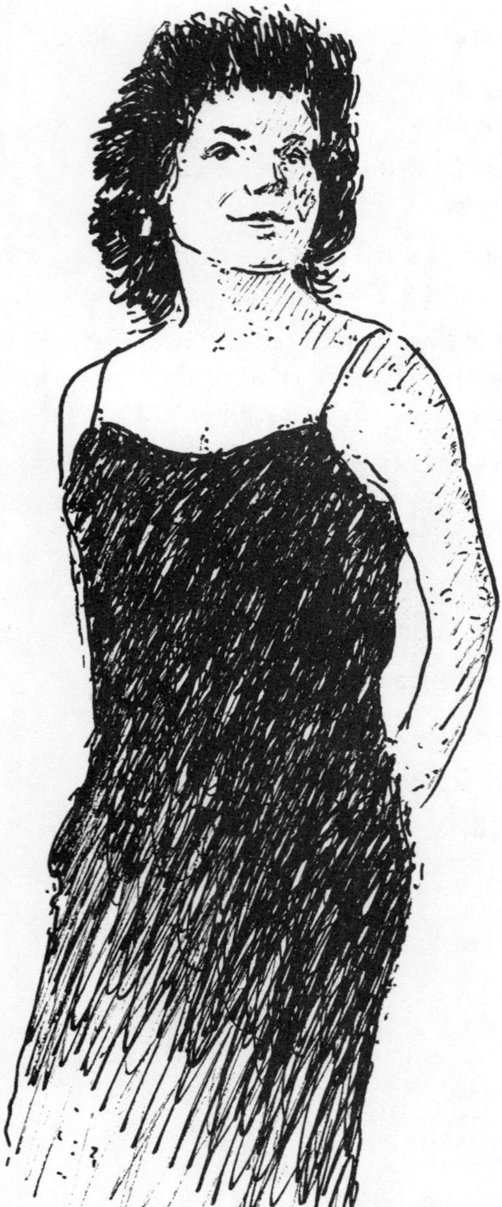

CHAPTER 7

The Script

"Survival, Elizabeth . . . we need to talk about survival."

She looked at me as if I were a stark, raving lunatic.

"I thought we were going to talk about my marriage."

"Your marriage, Elizabeth, is really only one facet on the gem, one bone in your body. It seems important now only because it's hurting."

She pondered that for a while, and then her face relaxed.

"I know it doesn't seem to make any sense to you now, but we need to talk about the person who's most important in your ideas about survival."

She gave me a statement she thought I wanted.

"I know, I know . . . I'm the most important person in my life . . . I'm responsible for my own happiness, it's my fault, uh. . . , " she tripped over the word, "responsibility."

She was not aware that she used such a self-incriminating tone.

"You stumbled on the word 'fault.' Do you think a lot of things are your fault . . . or responsibility?"

"Not really." She was being defensive, and she was lying.

"Anyway, I wasn't thinking of you when I mentioned the most important person in formulating your ideas about surviving. I was thinking about your 'poss.' "

"My poss?? What in heaven's name is a poss?"

She was smiling broadly and so was I.

Your poss is your P-O-S-S . . . parent of the same sex . . . your mother, Elizabeth, senior."

"Oh, no." She laughed at the joke. "We *have* to talk about her?"

"I'm afraid so. The parent of the same sex, your mother, obviously was the first living thing that you turned to in order to make sure you were okay as a baby. Kids are no different from other living organisms: they have an instinct to survive, and like to have reassurance, in any form, that they will. Your mother was the first mirror you looked into as a baby to see if you were going to make it through life, and, if I'm thinking along the right lines, she sent your reflections back to you in such a way as to make you feel less than capable of taking care of your own needs. Did you have any trouble pleasing your mother?"

"I couldn't do anything right for my mother." (Her words conveyed enormous understatement.) "No matter what I did, my older sister did it better, or it just wasn't good enough. My mother was a very forceful woman who always got her way. I'm sure she loved me, but she was so busy yelling and screaming at everybody . . . you know, I never really knew for sure. Even now when she calls every couple of days, I wonder what she's gonna' gripe about, and I get butterflies in my stomach."

I let Elizabeth's words fade out into the room. Silence for a few seconds and then I said,

"You needed a knight-in-shining-armor on a big white horse to come the rescue . . . "

She finished the sentence: " . . . to slay the ugly dragon?"

"Not so much to slay the dragon, as to insure your survival through life—to protect you against your own feelings of unworthiness."

She thought for a minute. "Is Mark my knight-in-shining-armor?" She was smiling almost mockingly.

The Script

"He's only one of them. I was thinking more along the lines of the first one—your father. Where was he?"

Elizabeth played right along with our little damsel-in-distress game and said,

"The ugly dragon scared him off. My parents were divorced when I was six."

"Do you see your father at all now?"

Elizabeth's face mellowed. "He lives alone in California, and I write him sometimes. When we get up there to see him, it's always a good time. He seems happy, but I can't help feeling sorry for him. My mother badmouths him to this day; it makes me so mad."

I stayed silent for a moment to see if she would say more. She looked a little confused.

"I know this has a lot to do with the trouble I'm having with Mark, but how does it connect? . . . I mean, the survival thing and all?"

I thought for a minute, looked around the room, then said, "We need to use a little analogy. It'll help you connect those two ideas, and give you an idea where we're going.

"Let's pretend that you're a little kid and you suddenly wake up in this darkened room with two silent strangers, A and B. When you awaken, you find yourself sitting closer to A, and you don't mind it because A, even in the shadows, seems to look more like you than B. Nothing much happens until someone yells through the walls that the building is on fire, and that it's every man for himself. You get scared when you see smoke coming under the only door out, so you turn to A for help and reassurance. A tells you, it's no use trying to make it, your're not capable enough. All the while A is really unsure of A's own ability to survive the situation.

"You realize now that your time is running out, so you turn to the other person in the room, B. B offers to help you out, saying there's nothing to worry about, but wants some reassurance that you really trust B before any help is given. You have no choice: B is your last hope for survival, so you shower B with love and do almost anything B asks. After all, you must keep B happy if you are to survive. As B helps you to prepare for your escape, B becomes your rescuer, savior, your knight-in-shining armor."

Elizabeth seemed intrigued by the little story, and I could see she was beginning to understand.

"A is my mother, and B is my father, right?"

"Correct, and that is why you love so hard in marriage—you see loving as a way of surviving, not as a way of experiencing joy."

She nodded and asked,

"What happened in the room after that?"

"B just couldn't seem to get things organized for the rescue. He would procrastinate. On top of that, A was yelling at him, telling him he was too weak and ineffective to help anybody get out. So there you were, smoke coming in under the door, A telling you that you were too stupid to get yourself out, A yelling at B and saying he was too weak to help, and you starting to get mad at B because he wouldn't take charge, tell A to shut up, and then rescue you."

Elizabeth was smiling. "There nothing like having a knight-in-shining-armor chicken out at the crucial time."

"That's exactly how you saw it, Elizabeth. B got so flustered that he got up, opened the door, and ran out into the smoke and flames without you. You passed out and woke up a while later; your mother was gone, but there was another stranger in the room, and his shadow looked a lot like B's. What do you think was the first thing that you did?"

Elizabeth grinned, "I did whatever he wanted to make him like me, right?"

"Exactly. That's called approval-seeking behavior: you do whatever necessary, even to the point of your own martyrdom and denial of joy, to get this new 'B' to like you enough to rescue you. Yet you don't trust him. After all, the first B ran out on you, so you need to test this new B to see if he's got what it takes to get you safely out of the burning building.

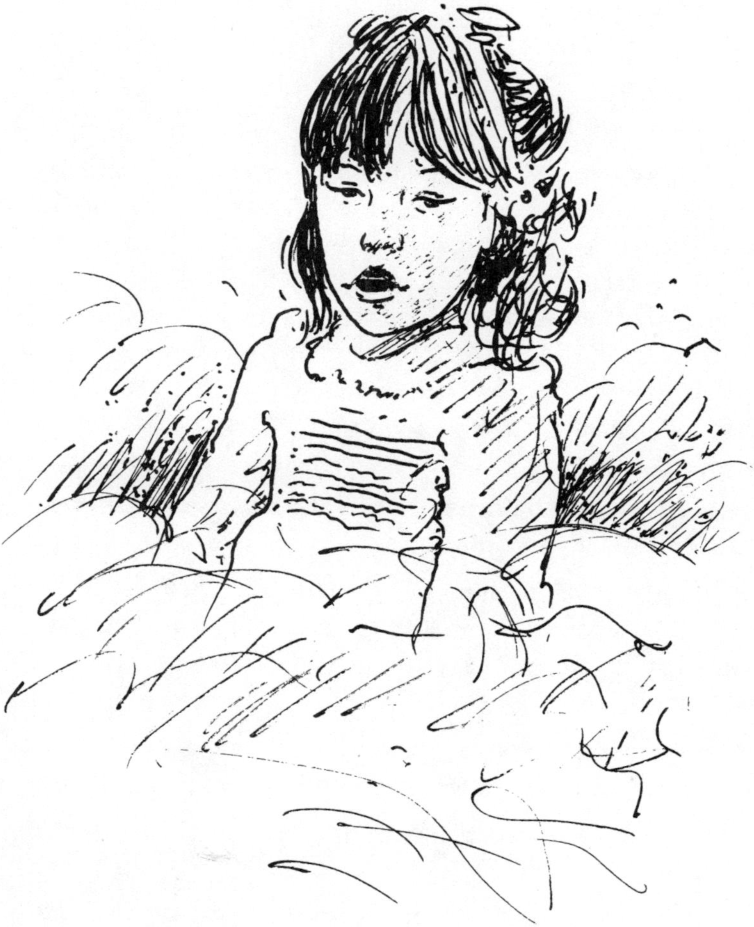

The only test you know is your mother's abusiveness, which scared off the first B. She's gone, so it's up to you to test this new B."

Elizabeth said, "So I really put him through the mill, just as my mother did, right?"

I nodded. "Whenever you feel any stress, insecurity, or anxiety about daily living—the smoke under the door—you unknowingly provoke a fight with Mark to see whether he'll stand up to you and take charge, or back down . . . It is truly a no-win situation for both of you: if he's forceful and takes charge, it reminds you of your weakness and vulnerability—your mother's horrid words echo in your ears. This recollection frightens you even more than the smoke. If Mark backs down, you get angry because the smoke and flames of life are licking at your feet and your knight-in-shining-armor is turning chicken, and you get angry and ask for a divorce."

Elizabeth grabbed the insight: "And I always stop short because the first man in my life ran out of me . . . "

I finished, " . . . and left you to die in the fire. Since you are convinced that you're totally incapable of rescuing yourself, you hang onto Mark. As angry as you get at him, you perceive it as a matter of absolute survival that he *stays*.

Elizabeth seemed relieved that the long story was over, and she smiled broadly at her new-found insight.

"All we have to do is convince me that I can get out of the room alive by myself . . . "

" . . . and you can experience the joy of loving someone you *want* to love, instead of needing to love him as if it were a matter of life and death."

She seemed overjoyed. "Great. How do we do that?"

"That's what the piano lessons are for, Elizabeth . . . that's what the piano lessons are for."

CHAPTER 8

New Beginnings

The session ended with a discussion of finances. I asked Elizabeth what her usual and customary fee was for a piano lesson, and she told me it was fifteen dollars for a half-hour. My fee was seventy-five dollars per session, so to make us square, Elizabeth would have to give my little friend John five lessons for each hour of psychotherapy.

I'm sure Elizabeth was starting to have some second thoughts about meeting John; after all, she really didn't understand why I was doing this, and the prospect of meeting someone new was not easy for her. Because of her tendency to be an approval-seeker, she would have to succeed in teaching this new person to play the piano, and thus get my blessing. It would be much easier to pay than to try to climb that mountain.

"I feel like this is worth it; I really can pay you the seventy-five dollars with no problem."

I understood, but I stood my ground.

"Elizabeth, I know these lessons are going to be a lot of trouble for you, much more than writing that check, but you've got to understand the lessons are really for your benefit . . . and I won't be able to explain why until we've had a few more sessions."

The real therapy was yet to come for Elizabeth in the piano lessons. She made an appointment for the following week, and left.

I called Boys Haven and made the arrangements for John's lessons; they would be once a week on Saturday morning at 10:30. Later that week the house-parent told me that John was very excited about the lessons and had even refused a home visit with his father on Saturday. Apparently John was beginning to realize, at the age of eleven, that if neither A nor B was going to help him out of that smoky room, he ought to give serious consideration to other people—strangers, myself, and especially Elizabeth. She was, at this point, nameless, faceless, and sexless to John, but other than myself, was the first person in a long time to care genuinely about his well-being.

Saturday morning was rainy and cold, and with my nose against the living room window I could strain my neck to see Elizabeth and Mark's house. Right on time, the house-parent pulled the Chevy Suburban up to the drive, and John jumped out. He was wearing a Dallas Cowboys windbreaker that was one of my early icebreakers with him.

As the half-hour dragged on, I wondered with intense curiosity what was going on over there. I knew Elizabeth would never find the exact words to describe the growth of her feelings for John, but I knew from my own experience that such simple acts outside the mainstream of one's life could start a sublime chain of events.

When the half-hour was up, I watched out the window, my neck crooked, but John didn't come out—Elizabeth was keeping him a little longer. It must have been twenty minutes later—my neck was stiff from being in such a cocked position—when John came out and got into the Suburban. He was carrying something, and when they drove by my front door, I could see that it was a cookie.

Nothing signficiant to the casual observer, but my stiff neck was mute testimony to the fact that I was more than a casual observer. I'm sure many piano teachers offer their eleven-year-old students a cookie or two, but the act of feeding has a sub-connotation in our society of nurturing and loving. Indeed, this was the source of Elizabeth's weight problem—She felt un-nurtured and unloved by her over-critical mother and weak, ineffective father. Her eating was simply her way of giving love to herself.

And, just perhaps, by such a common gesture, Elizabeth was beginning to love John.

Then again, maybe I was reaching a bit.

△   ▽   △

I did not see Elizabeth for her second appointment; she cancelled without speaking to me and didn't reschedule. A lot of patients who are ambivalent about changing their lives do this. They get an idea about what is wrong in their lives, and the insight is a temporary narcotic. They are afraid to upset the precarious balance of good feelings they have until the next crisis occurs and they go back to square one.

Elizabeth was doing this, I knew, but it was simply a human weakness. I myself never go to the dentist unless I have a toothache—not wise behavior, but human—and Elizabeth was doing the same thing. There would be another storm, the play would be re-enacted with the usual ending, and Elizabeth would be back.

That Saturday the lesson ran through lunch, and afterwards I saw Elizabeth give John a ride back in her car.

Sunday was a fine day, and much of the neighborhood was out cleaning up the last of autumn's litter. Typically Sunday was a day when the inhabitants of our little city clung together; there was always a certain dread in the air because Monday was lurking. It was late in the afternoon when Mark sauntered over to speak.

"Boy, I don't know what you're doing with that woman, but she sure has changed."

His smile was half-hearted. I wondered if he thought I practiced voodoo.

"Well, Mark, I don't think I could have done that much; Elizabeth's had only one session."

Mark stalled for a few seconds, as if he were really thinking.

"Well, that little feller sure has hit it off with Liz. She just can't do enough for him."

"... butting in on your territory, Mark?"

We laughed a while about that, but the conversation faded, and is face got serious.

"Well, we lost a son eight years ago to cancer, and Liz and I've been having a lotta trouble ever since. I wonder if she doesn't blame herself for what happened."

"That's partly it. What's really going on is a little complicated, but Elizabeth likes to mother everybody because it makes her feel strong. It's like worrying about whether you're able to change a tire on your car, until one dark night when you stop and help somebody else change a flat—then your confidence is shored up."

Mark though for a second. "You're right; it is a little complicated."

I continued. "When your son died, Elizabeth needed to feel strong, so she turned to mothering you to give her strength. That's when the trouble started. If my guess is correct, you and your mother weren't the best of friends."

Mark smiled defensively. "My mother was one of the toughest broads I ever knew. She drove the old man to drink; he'd come home drunk, beat us kids up, and pass out. If the ld lady woulda' left him alone, he never woulda' been a drunk."

I let merciful silence take over for a few seconds.

"Mark, tell Elizabeth to come back. She really needs a few more sessions to get the whole picture ... and let her have all the time she wants with John—he's keeping it peaceful around your place."

"Sure, Doc ... sure."

As I raked, I thought. Every time Elizabeth felt anxious or insecure she reassured herself of her ability to make it by mothering people around her. When her son died and her daughter was an adolescent busy rebelling against any mothering, Elizabeth *needed* people to mother, so she naturally chose Mark. Each time after that, when stress occurred and she needed to mother him, she would spark the bad memories of his own mother, and the trouble would start.

In her time of stress, Elizabeth wanted Mark to act strong, and when he tried, she would be reminded of how weak she was. Unconsciously blaming her mother for these feelings of weakness, she would lash out at Mark and this anger would start a replay of his own childhood with his shrewish, angry mother. Fearing that he would lose the approval of Elizabeth, the mother-figure, and thus jeopardize his own feelings of well-being, Mark would back down from Elizabeth and, of course, this reminded Elizabeth of her weak and ineffective father. More anger. More trouble.

Mark was right: it was complicated. But it went on in every marriage to some hidden degree, and it boiled down to the fact that Elizabeth was paying for the sins of Mark's mother, and Mark was paying for the sins of Elizabeth's father.

It was a love debt that went on forever.

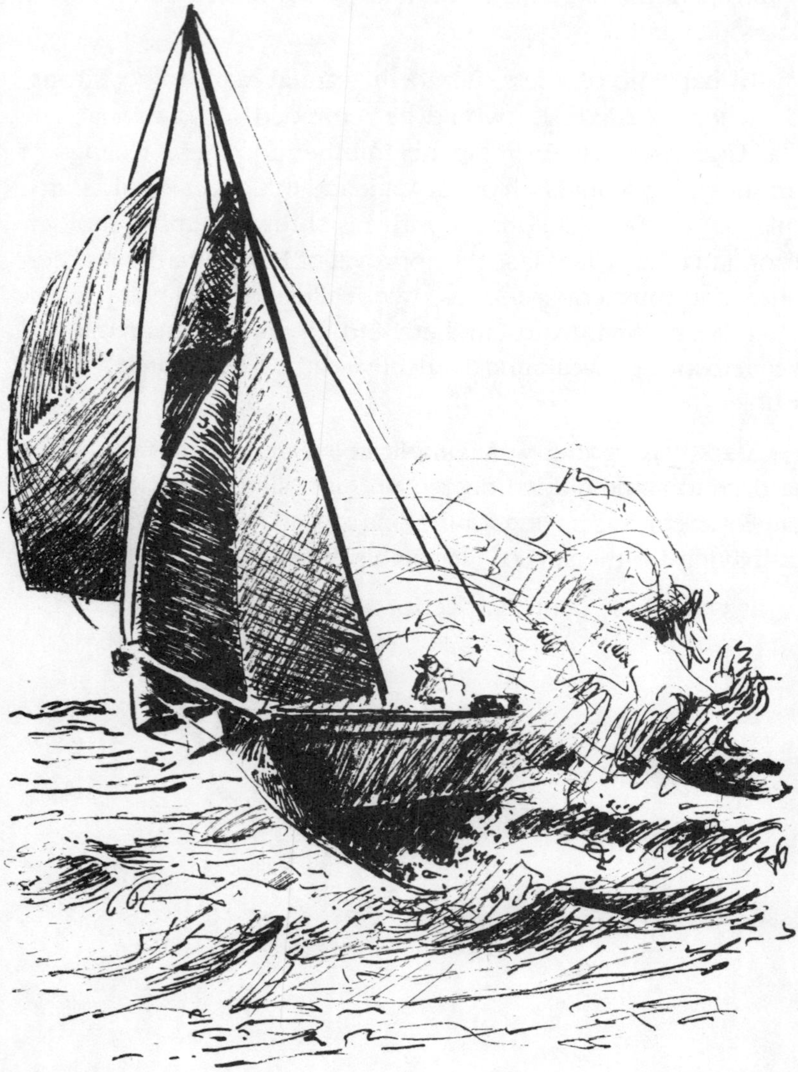

CHAPTER 9

Storm and Calm

Elizabeth didn't call that week, and while I knew there was temporary calm, I feared the storm was just around the corner.

It was the Saturday before Thanksgiving, and with less fervor than before, I watched to see if John was still coming for his lessons. Happily, he was, but on this particular day, he didn't come in the house-parent's Suburban. He was driven by an older boy who used the administrator's old Ford.

The older boy was sixteen, and apparently newly licensed, for he drove rather slowly. His name was Walter, and I knew him fairly well. He had never impressed me as being mechanically able, and I worried about the safety of the two boys, unsupervised in a car. Yet I was sure whoever let them use the car was confident of their good judgment—certainly there was no cause for concern about Walter's having the necessary driving skills to be a hot-rodder.

Walter was a lovable, freckle-faced kid, who appeared and acted younger than his years, but who had just as many horror stories under his skin as John.

Like Mark, Walter had had a strong, survivor-type mother figure and a weak, ineffective father. Walter's real mother had walked out on a husband and four kids under the age of 12. She apparently had had enough floor-scrubbing, toilet-cleaning, cooking, and wet-nursing for four children—five including her husband—and she simply packed a few clothes and crossed the state line into the Louisiana badlands.

Walter's father was not to remain un-nurtured for long, however. He quickly married a strong, organized woman who was also conveniently a parole officer. She quickly provided clean floors and toilets, hot meals, and plenty of organized discipline. Walter, the second oldest puppy in her inherited litter, did not like her one bit. He expressed his displeasure about this new mom to his father by taking things that weren't his, especially coins and small bills from his stepmother's purse.

The stepmother felt this boy needed some effective discipline and, in the truest spirit of the American penal tradition, locked him in his room, and allowed him out only to go the bathroom and for school. When he behaved for a few days, he was allowed normal privileges. Walter had a point to prove, however, and soon coins and small bills once again disappeared from the jailer's purse.

Certainly, the frustration felt by this woman is something that has touched all of us who inherit somebody else's kids, and she was by no means abusive. She was just trying to save child psychologist's fees and keep parking-meter money in her purse.

Walter, however, saw it differently. He was sure his story would make page-one headlines in *The National Enquirer,* and when it didn't Walter embellished it and then spread it all over town.

That's how Walter wound up at Boys Haven—a place where he neither felt abused nor found purses lying about.

Yet it wasn't this woman who bothered Walter so much. In fact, I believe that after their little stalemate, they had a healthy respect for one another. What really bothered Walter was the fact that his father, his flesh-and-blood image of himself, had never once come to his rescue.

Still another victim of the absent knight-in-shining-armor, Walter sat in the car waiting for John to come out. Fate is a parsimonious parent to us when it comes to miracles, but one was about to take place. Mark pulled into the drive next to Walter and stared for a few minutes, with the appropriate curiosity of one finding a strange kid staked out in front. Walter, I'm sure, saw an opportunity to embellish and lavish his story upon yet another pair of ears.

I found out later that this was exactly what happened. Two souls, both allegedly having suffered at the hands of strong women, and both without shining knights, compared notes as they stood in the driveway, oblivious to a biting November wind.

Inside, meanwhile, two other souls were learning how to be mother and son again.

Walter and Mark talked for a good while, until John came out; then the boys left, Walter struggling to find second gear as they drove past my door.

As they left, they looked happy. It was with good reason: on that next Thursday, the Thanksgiving table at Elizabeth and Mark's was set for four. The wheels of a machine about which I knew very little were starting to turn—wheels that were running on parallel tracks through several people's lives.

△ ▽ △

It was the first of December when Elizabeth made the appointment. The storm between her and Mark had no doubt occurred, but this time I agreed to see her only if she promised to keep regular follow-up appointments.

When I saw her, I could tell at once that something different was happening. Elizabeth had lost considerable weight in the month of her absence. Sitting in front of me was a beautiful woman who had shed her matronliness.

There was no nervous chatter this time; she was upset, quietly so, because she and Mark had had a rather severe quarrel. Elizabeth felt that Mark was not adjusting to the change in her.

"I really don't understand why we fought, everything was going so well—you know with the boys and all."

I listened intently, looking for hidden meanings behind her words and gestures, but there were none.

"Elizabeth, I know you're feeling bad, but these troubles you're having with Mark are really right on schedule. I need to explain a couple more ideas so that you'll understand why you and Mark clash so much. I'd like to talk today about something I call, 'paying the love debt.' "

Elizabeth managed a weak joke. "I know it was my fault."

"No, I'm afraid we all carry a love debt around with us. Some of us take this debt very seriously, as if our lives depended on it. Others of us pay little mind to it, and still others pay it back with a vengeance. Sometimes we use our lovers and spouses as ways of making time-payments on our debt."

She listened, and then asked, "Sounds interesting, but what is this 'love debt'?"

I plunged in.

"Originally, psychologists thought that we learned to love primarily by watching our parents, and if we perceived any hint of injustice in that relationship, we carried away a need to make that injustice right—a kind of love debt."

She wasn't yet understanding one thing I was saying, but I continued.

"For instance, let us suppose a young man grows up watching his father mistreat his mother—the degree is not important here; it could be physical beatings or emotional deprivation—in most instances he carries away a sense of the unjust lot of women. If his mother gave him any nurturing at all, and we can safely assume that she did, and if his father was at all nasty toward him, and we can also assume this happened because abusive behavior usually spreads laterally, then the young man is going to feel a certain alliance with his mother. This alliance represens to him a need to undo as much of the mistreatment as he can, and it becomes closely linked to his mother's nurturing. The young man sees it as a kind of business deal: she gives me nurturing (feeds me, clothes me, wipes my nose) and I have to undo her pain from my father. Later on, this notion gets turned around: if I want nurturing and loving from the opposite sex, then I have to undo their suffering."

Elizabeth was beginning to understand. "It all sounds so logical; I just wish I could remember it all."

I reassured her with warning.

"There's much more to it than that. We really don't just learn to love from watching our parents. The whole learning process is actually a collection of many of our life-experiences which develops into what I call the Romantic Ideal: the sum total of what we want from loving other people.

"Our expectations about love come not just from watching our parents interact and create the love debt, but also from our exposure to other people, the movies, TV, books, songs, and especially commercial advertisements. As we bump along through life, the intensity of our love debt and of our romantic expectations may change, increase, and even go away, depending on the person we interact with. In your case, Mark happens to be very pliable, having a love debt of his own, and this circumstance places you both in the position of playing out the injustices of your love debts against each other. Tell me, have you recovered from the death of your son?"

Elizabeth's face didn't change much, and she seemed matter-of-fact about her answers.

"When my son died, I tried to cling to Mark, but he just was never there when I needed him. I got so furious with him, I lashed out at him every chance I got."

"Do you understand why you did that?"

"I guess . . . I needed him."

"More than that, you blamed yourself. Do you remember your smoky room, with A and B in it? Your son's death restated your mother's very vocal opinions about your abilities: not only couldn't you not get yourself out of that burning building to survive, you failed at keeping your child alive."

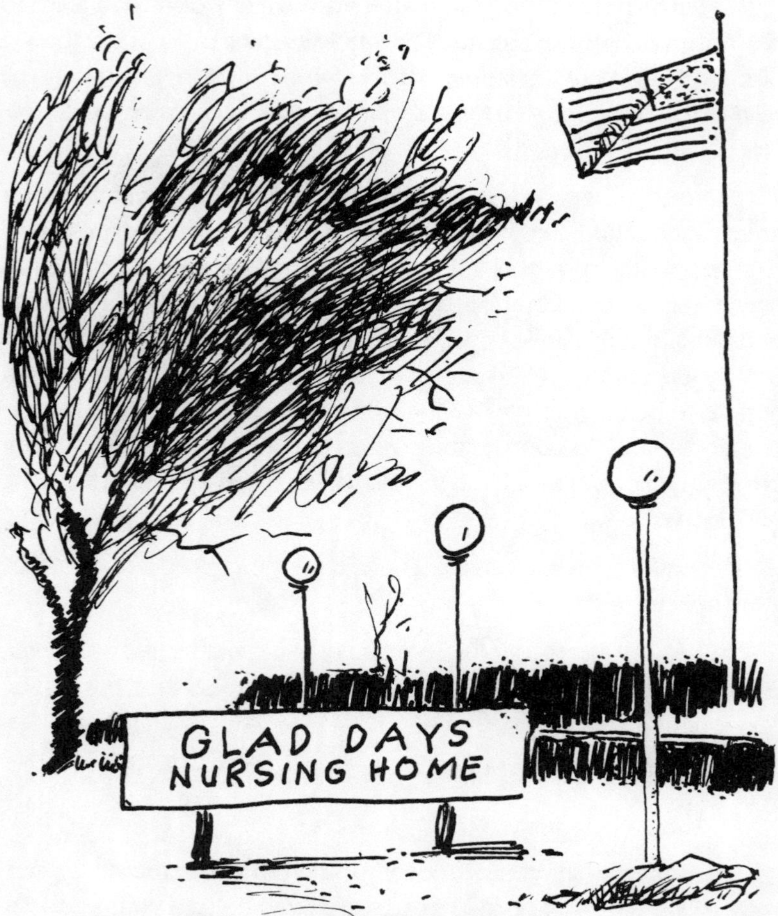
GLAD DAYS
NURSING HOME

Her eyes filled with tears, and I grabbed her hands and held them tight.

"When that happened, you were really convinced you'd never get out of that smoky room alone, and with the panic of death choking at you, you turned to B, Mark, the other shadow in the room. And to make him help you out of the room, you lavished him with attention and approval-seeking behavior.

"Mark interprets any such behavior from a woman as a sort of mothering. Since he had so much trouble with his own mother, he accepted your nurturing warily, and was a little afraid to give any back. Unknowingly, he then replayed the passive, useless role of your cowardly father. This made you furious, and the fights you provoked once again replayed Mark's unfortunate relationship with his mother."

Elizabeth felt better, but looked a little dazed. She said, "Gosh, no matter what you do to kids, you really mess 'em up, huh?"

"No, Elizabeth. Everyone has a love debt. You and Mark just happen to be pliable enough to be good actors in the replays, and just happen to have the right keys for the right locks to open the floodgates."

She relaxed a bit, and I continued.

"It's all gotten much worse in the last half-century. Movies, TV ads—all have given us such unrealistic hopes for our love debts to go away—and when they don't, we seek more escapism, and our expectations get even more unrealistic."

She asked, "What is Mark's love debt?"

"Mark sees his parent of the opposite sex as the critical, nasty bad guy how tells him he won't get out of the smoky room. Mark's father dealt with the harshness of the mother by being a drunk, so Mark couldn't turn to him for help. Mark knew that he would have to deal with the smoky room—life—as well as people of the opposite sex, in his own way. Sometimes he has chosen his father's way of drinking too much, and sometimes he has contrived his own solutions—that's why he's such a good salesman.

"Mark's love debt is that he sees men, and thus himself, as suffering at the hands of nasty mothers, who do nothing for them except tell them over and over again how useless they are. This kind of debt is paid with *revenge*. Mark's loving tends to be cold, calculating, and practical. He'll accept your nurturing, approval-seeking, and mothering, but if you stop or get made, you'll feel the sharp edge of his vengeance. It may be a slap across the face, neglect at social gatherings, staying out late with the guys drinking, and even mindless, emotionless, one-night-stands with an easy bar pick-up."

Elizabeth stared off for a while, as if thinking of the past, then slowly smiled.

"It all makes sense."

I let the silence fill the room for a good while. She asked what the piano lessons were for. I told her they bolstered up her image of herself as a person who not only could survive but could help another survive. Much more than this, John represented the ultimate unmothered (and unfathered) individual who could tap into Elizabeth's abundant need to seek approval and mother the world. When Elizabeth felt confident and strong, she would be able to deal with Mark on a more equal basis, and the parent-punishing plays they staged would no longer be necessary. Their love debt would fade away.

Besides, it made me feel good to see John play the piano. I might need him someday to come and play for me at the Old Folks home. And maybe John would *need to do just that*.

CHAPTER 10

A New Christmas Story

What was the magic worked by the two cast-off boys? They were busy working nothing short of a miracle on two very average adults suffering in their loving as we all do.

We know of John's role. We know how this frail boy has been a repository for Elizabeth's nurturing: how he has been receptive to her warmth and caring without qualification or hope of secondary gain. He has allowed Elizabeth to love again without paying a price for it.

But what of Walter? How has he worked his magic on the frightened, self-protecting Mark?

Wlater, by Fate's kind hand, just happened to fit Mark's profile of suffering. Both were failed by a weak, ineffective father who never stepped in and stood up for the child against a punitive mother. Walter offered Mark a very important blackboard on which Mark could not only draw himself, but also erase and rewrite. And it all happened so naturally: rainy Saturdays on the basketball court, Tuesday evening bowling lessons, video games after frequent dinner visits.

Walter allowed Mark to be the father neither one of them ever had. When Mark was a good father to Walter, it braced both of them with hope that such people do exist. As Walter would come to fall in and out

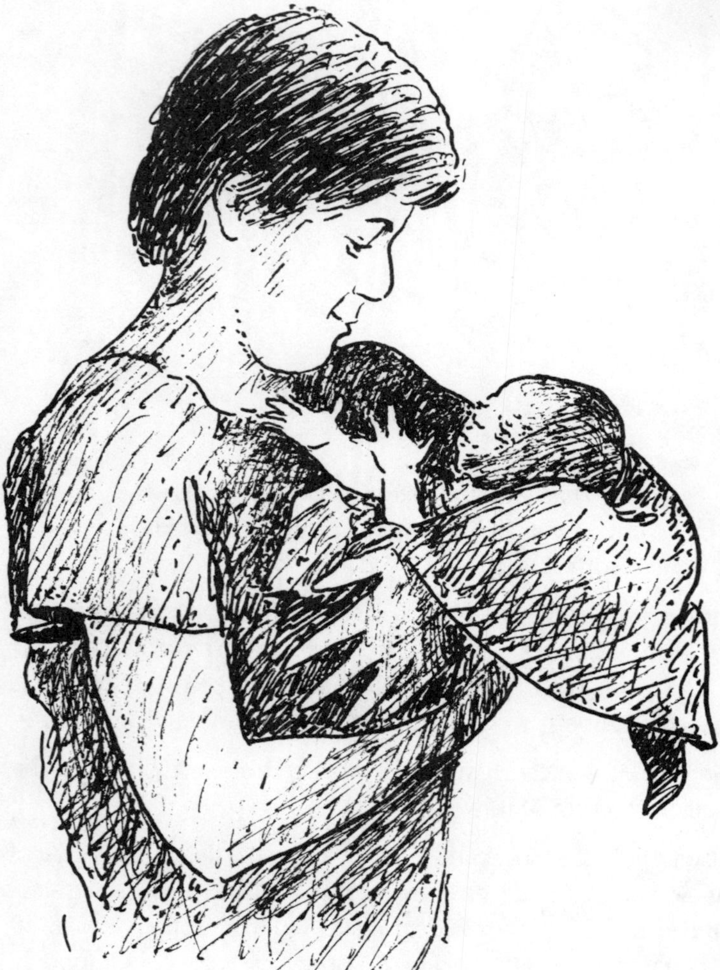

of love, the two men would watch their attitudes toward women change together. Mark would say: "Be careful, Walter, remember the beast." And Walter would say, "No, this one's different." Both would learn not only that there are many different kinds of women, but that women are people who need warmth, tenderness, and understanding just as much as men do.

Mark would learn that money is only a means to an end, and that Walter's feelings might be more important than some shyster land deal. So Mark would come to see himself in a better light as a result of helping Walter, and he, too, would learn to love without paying a price.

Christmas Eve, Boys Haven, Middleton Cottage:

I remember that there were perhaps ten boys there, John and Walter among them. These two were to spend part of the Christmas holidays with Elizabeth and Mark. This night was their official time to receive gifts supplied by the Board of Directors and many loving volunteers.

The festivities were in full swing. Packages were being torn open with glee. Tears of joy were being shed by volunteers who had worked hard all year. And then, like a warm fire, the party was beginning to die down.

Elizabeth, Mark, and Walter were waiting for John.

He was out on the porch in near-freezing temperatures, waiting for the old rusting Ford and his old rusting knight. John's father was supposed to come and give him a gift before his departure with Mark and Elizabeth.

John was such a frail figure sitting huddled up on the stoop. I thought a scene like this was corny enough in movies, but here it was in real life: the little match boy, waiting for the glowing angel in white to make him whole again.

As the hour grew late, the scene became more pathetic. Elizabeth went out and sat next to John on the cold concrete, while I watched discreetly through the window.

When it became obvious that his knight-in-shining-armor had failed him once again, John broke down and wept heaving sobs. And in a scene as touching as any I have ever witnessed, Elizabeth took John and held him to her breast. I think she knew at last there is no point in waiting for rescue by white knights— that, in fact, we don't need them. She may have told John that instead of prancing horses and shining knights, there are only Elizabeths.

Or perhaps she sang it:

. . . Hush, little baby, don't say a word,
Daddy's gonna buy you a mockingbird . . .

Part III

CHAPTER 11

The Survival Plan

Beginnings: The End of the Free Ride

I am about to describe it, at considerable length, how love relationships and, to a lesser degree, other relationships are formulated around our instinct to live.

In the phrase "survival plan," the second word is aptly chosen. Our will to live is a complex blueprint, a computer program (to be more timely) of many different forces. The word "survival" itself has a meaning that goes beyond the traditional usage of "staying alive." In medical texts, it means "to stay alive past" some life-threatening event. For example, a cancer patient who has shown no sign of recurrence five years after discovery of the disease may be said to have "survived."

What is the event in our physiological and emotional development beyond which mere staying alive becomes (in an almost Darwinian sense) a struggle for survival? It is birth. Prenatally we are in every sense dependent on our mothers. Physiologically, our warmth, our shelter and protection, our oxygenation, our nourishment, our waste disposal, our defense against disease—and even perhaps our moods—are taken freely.

From such a free ride, then, in which everything is provided for us, we are stripped of our complacency by birth, beyond which we must undertake our first major task: a gasp for air. The word "survival" now takes on its enhanced meaning of "staying alive beyond" the trauma of our first separation.

Starting from birth and continuing throughout our lives, we formulate and reformulate a basic outline of all our needs and wants. This plan of action is structured around and fueled by a core, and that core is the basic instinct to survive in all living creatures. The survival plan is expanded and modified by our life's experiences, and especially by the people we encounter. The survival plan of a person who has spent part of his or her life in a war zone will have a very different shape from that of someone who has always been sheltered and protected.

The survival plan idea is important for us because we tend to form many of our relationships with others—romantic love, friendships, business associations, fondness for children and pets—by "casting" others into roles that play out a scenario for us. Our survival plan determines the plot of this play, which is a running, day-to-day script for our lives. The strength, substance, and credibility of the plot are determined by how much faith we have in ourselves.

We've all seen movies and TV shows with weak plots, and realized the experience was not fulfilling because we just didn't see those events as following logically from one another. If our survival plan is weak, we feel insecure about our ability to make it through life because the events in our story just don't seem true-to-life either.

When you look closely at your survival plan, then, a prime consideration will be just how believable and realistic the plot is.

I am reminded of a young woman named Arlene who grew up watching her mother cook, clean, and do housework. Through all the toil, the mother managed a few smiles, but for the most part seemed resigned to the situation as her lot in life.

"At least I have a roof over my head," she would say.

As all of us grow up, we formulate a plan for survival based on mimicking our parents of the same sex provided that the plan to be copied looks appealing. In this case, however, Arlene, in planning her life, decided quite unconsciously that she wanted no part of scrubbing floors because it was clear that her mother's life wasn't much fun. Arlene made a quiet commitment to herself that her plan for living would include some kind of career—any career, as long as she didn't have to be a housewife stuck at home.

The career Arlene finally chose was banking. It seemed, after all, a stable and honorable profession that might provide a good chance for advancement. Everyone applauded Arlene's choice as sensible and realistic. Yet for the young woman to feel good about her goal, she needed to feel confident in her own ability to succeed. She needed to *believe* she possessed the strength of self to be a good banker.

Unfortunately for Arlene, self-strength, self-confidence, feelings of adequacy, a good self-image—all these were problematic. The young woman's mother had not been terribly happy, or at least had not shown as much to her daughter. And yet the mother had stayed with her "lot in life" for all the years the daughter had known her. Since the young woman did not perceive her mother as being strong and assertive, she herself was unable to mimic a strong sense of self-worth. It is a common enough pattern that unhappy parents unwittingly reinforce this lack of confidence in their children of the same sex.

So Arlene entered the banking world full of excitement and enthusiasm about her new career, but also with rumblings of insecurity. As each new challenge came up, she felt a great deal of anxiety; her own small mistakes devastated her. She was not sure she possessed the personal raw material for the job because she did not find the plot of her survival play especially believable as written.

Arlene had several options at this point. All of them centered on bringing in other people to shore up her survival plot and make it more believable to her. If Arlene had been very lucky, she might have come across a female bank executive higher up the corporate ladder than she, who could give enough constructive criticism, praise, and encouragement to make her believe in herself. Such an occurrence cannot be counted on, however, as people higher up success's ladder often fear losing their jobs to those on the lower rungs.

Finding herself at the beginning of a new career without adequate emotional support from family or work associates, Arlene turned to her love life to look for the knightly savior. She sought out stronger men and "wrote" them into her survival play to give the plot some substance. As in an old Errol Flynn movie, the plot was weak, the leading lady was in trouble, and a swashbuckling hero was required to save the day.

The seeking-out of strong men takes place very automatically and very unconsciously. Many young women find themselves attracted to men who have some of the qualities our society defines as "dominant": tallness, wealth, expensive tastes and the means to gratify them, an age and experience of life beyond their own.

Arlene, however, was already married to a man of "lesser strength" whom she had met at a stage in life before her desire for a career became paramount. She was in the unhappy situation of being married to a man whose own capacity to cope and win through seemed problematic. As a result, the daily challenges of her job became portents of failure in her career. This fear of failure was unconscious, of course, as was her fear of the alternative to her career—being an unhappy housewife like her mother.

In a situation in which all available options seemed unacceptable, Arlene found herself attracted to "stronger" men outside her marriage. For the first time in her life, she toyed with the idea of having an extramarital affair.

Extramarital affairs are usually quite intense. The romantic and sexual interplay in these relationships are described by many as being "higher than any high," and with good reason: the act of sexual coupling is done purely for self-gratification.

Arlene's fantasies came to follow a script something like this:

1. "I need to see myself as strong in order to feel secure in my life."

2. "I feel that I am capable of surviving when important people tell me I'm worthwhile."

3. "My husband's opinions of me are not helpful because I don't see him as being strong and important."

4. "My lover is strong and important."

5. "He tells me I am worthy of his time, affection, and love."

6. "He proves to me that I am worthwhile with flowers, phone calls, and lovemaking."

Thus every phone call, every sexual interlude is seen as a vivid reinforcement of the woman's capacity to survive—a form of "borrowed strength."

There are, however, several problems with this logic. First is the obvious contradiction: if the lover gives the woman strength simply by phoning her, then he takes away strength when he doesn't phone. That is why such a relationship has a potential to cause so much emotional turmoil. Moreover, while some degree of "borrowing strength" may be perfectly healthy, it becomes unhealthy and painful when it is the *only* source of self-strength. Such a relationship is inherently volatile and painful because it is based on *need* rather than *want*.

The person who throws you a life-ring on a stormy sea is your savior only if he or she holds on and pulls you in. Seen from any angle, such a "rescue" is a risky business. As Arlene had to learn through experience, the only sure survival plan would be one she engineered, reinforced, and carried out herself.

Two Survival Plans That Spelled Doom

Our neighborhood is certainly not an uncommon place: it is a suburb with clean streets and single-story brick houses too close together. The people here all make a decent living, but with the cost of things these days, a lot live on the outer fringe of financial solvency. When the recession hit and settled down in our area, the mailman, a bit of a gossip, talked of all the bounced checks and collection notices he'd delivered that week by certified mail.

Our town is one of those Southern boom-towns where almost all the economic blood flows along a single artery. When the recession cut that artery, the town suffered very badly. Virtually every business was affected, even the medical business. I knew of only two businesses that did fairly well during the hard times: the florists and, of course, the merchants of distilled spirits. It seemed strange to me that florists could still sell dispensable luxuries like cut flowers when a lot of people had to use their Master Charge to buy food. Perhaps the flowers were reminders of good times past, or symbols of good times to come. Or maybe the flowers were the last dying breath of denial that the survival plan had somehow failed.

Thinking of that time and place, I am reminded of Barry and Monica. My first recollection is of a good-looking couple, the kind that enhance the decor at summer parties. They weren't especially loud, either, and this quality, combined with their looks, made them much in demand in the neighborhood.

Barry, a tall blond man of about forty-two, was a salesman for a tool company. The recession seemed to have taken its toll and cut him back far below what he was used to living on. Monica was fifteen years his junior, a pretty woman with two kids from another marriage.

I discovered their secrets by getting Monica drunk one afternoon. Now don't get me wrong—it was not an intentional ruse. Monica came over to borrow an extension cord. She seemed so terribly anxious to talk to someone that I offered her a drink. Having absolutely no tolerance for alcohol, she wound up giving me her whole life's story, along with Barry's. I was a somewhat reluctant but compassionate listener.

Many months later, after they had split up and moved, I thought of their stories and realized they both had had well-developed survival plans, each complementary to the other's needs. There was no suspicion of the doom that was to come. Theirs was the story of two perfectly good ideas about living that didn't work together.

Barry's father, Monica told me, was a serious man with little to say, but he taught Barry well that the best way to survive in this world is through hard work. The father's lack of warmth was made up for by Barry's mother, who offered the boy ample nurturing and protection when things got tough. This all seemed normal enough, but Barry's parents were worriers who constantly and verbally fretted about money. Barry frequently saw his father go on a tirade of cursing his mother for a carelessly spent dollar or two.

Barry's survival plan was focused well enough around hard work, but his parents' frequent fights over money left Barry with the firm resolve that he would *always* have enough money, no matter how hard he had to work. He saw his mother suffer because of the lack of money, and since his mother was his sole source of nurturing and emotional support, money became his primary goal in surviving. It was as if he were left with the idea that he could buy nurturing and emotional support, because he saw his parents at peace only when there was a surplus of cash.

Monica herself lost her father to divorce when she was six, and it didn't seem surprising that she had chosen both past and present husbands because of their strength and fondness for making money. She and her younger sister had been raised by their mother, and they all had had a rough time financially. The bad times ended when her mother married a man with some money and a stable business, but when he ran off with his secretary, the mother and daughters were once again in financial trouble. When Monica was a teenager, her mother remarried for a third time, and financial harmony made Monica's last years at home pleasant ones.

Monica's ideas about making it through life were formulated by her view of her mother and her mother's three marriages. The survival plan was based on marriage to men who made a good living. This was not such an unhealthy idea by itself, but for Monica its reverse side governed a lot of her behavior:

1. "I will survive and be happy if I marry a man with a good income."

2. "I will *not* survive and will *not* be happy if I don't marry a man with a good income."

So for Monica, marriage wasn't a state in life in which to share joyful experiences with someone; it was a lifeline, the only way to live. When her first husband felt that he was needed more than he was wanted, he sought refuge in another woman, and unwittingly replayed the horror story of Monica's first stepfather.

So Monica didn't waste time when she found out her first husband was having an affair. She dumped him without a great deal of remorse and set out to find a new power source for her survival plan. She and Barry were married less than eight months after her divorce.

The marriage, although not founded on the most ideal of motives, ran along rather smoothly at first. Barry was often too wrapped up in his money-making schemes and investments to worry about Monica's needing him rather than wanting him; as long as the money flowed, Barry's emotional needs were met. Monica immersed herself in her kids; as long as Barry had a job, she felt things would be fine. Monica never took the time to develop any closeness with Barry: her survival plot was playing

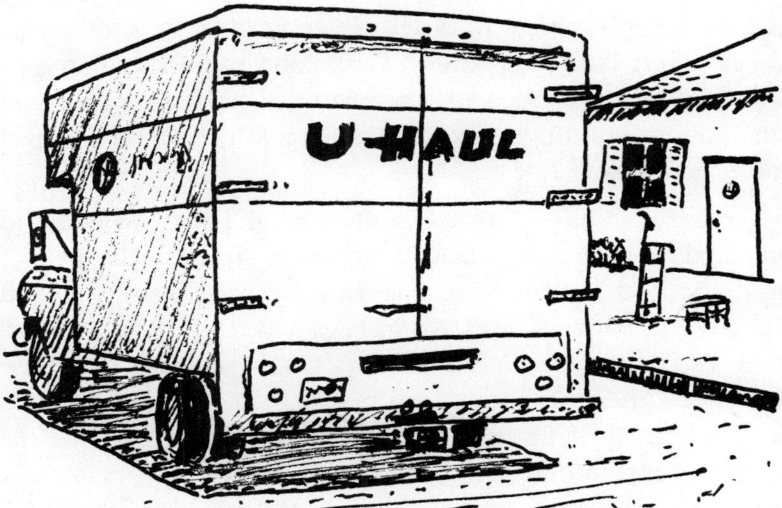
U-HAUL

out correctly and there was little need for serious, soul-shaking intimacy.

When the recession hit our town, both Monica's and Barry's plans began to buckle. As business dropped off, Barry's income fell by two-thirds. He was so paralyzed with disbelief and fear that he was unable to think clearly, and he sat at home many days drinking scotch. His money had been too good for too long; he refused to accept the fact that he had to lower his standard of living, and he thus didn't try to compensate for the drop in business with longer hours or harder work.

As he became more concerned about their finances, Monica unconsciously began to "see" a vivid dramatization of her bad times as a child. Barry seemed to be losing his job, and since Monica's survival plan was built around marriage to a man with a good job, she began to express discontent with his lack of enthusiasm. She understood neither her own feelings nor his. Because her own survival was important to her, and because they had not taken the time to develop a more sharing relationship, she gave very little sympathy and emotional support to Barry. As a child, Barry was used to a woman's nurturing and support when things got tough, and the combination of Monica's anger and rejection was a death blow.

I knew all this, of course, only after the fact. No one was prepared for the appearance of a U-Haul truck in the neighborhood at a late hour one Saturday night. Over the next few days, the news spread that Monica and her kids had moved back with her mother in Austin; Barry would stay until the house was sold. When people split up in a neighborhood as close as ours, especially if there is no clearly apparent reason for the divorce, everybody feels personally hurt—and personally vulnerable. People seem to feel that divorce is an ogre who chooses families at random and knocks on the door. (With some such irrational terror medieval villagers must have viewed the bubonic plague.)

I wondered, a few months after Barry and Monica were gone, whether the separation could have been avoided. Each of them needed not merely self-strength; they needed whole new survival plans, completely refurbished plots of their future lives.

Both of them could have been helped by nurturing and caring behavior as a therapeutic measure, but this type of therapy would have to have been structured differently for each. For Barry, there would have been Boys Haven—its gym was open seven days a week, and there were always boys in there looking for a little one-on-one. Even in our small town, there were three separate Boys Clubs desperately in need of volunteers for all kinds of projects; two of them had Big Brother programs. One or two hours a week of this type of activity would have given Barry an augmented sense of self-strength, a boost that would have vividly demonstrated his hidden resources. If he had seen himself as having the creative energy to help a few youngsters, then perhaps he would have believed that he possessed the creative energy to help helself. More important, Barry would have seen that he could engage in a meaningful activity without getting paid for it. He could have seen that harmony, closeness, and sharing don't come only when money flows.

Yet this ogre we fear, this monster who threatens our family bonds, doesn't live outside our front gate. It lives inside our homes. It is, in essence, our relationships. Unless we love from a position of self-strength, we will always be potential victims of the ogre and of late-night U-Haul trucks.

Revising Monica's survival plan would have been a little more complicated. She certainly would have felt greater self-strength from nurturing and caring behavior, but what she really needed to learn was a sense of independence from men. A job might have done the trick; her children were in school, and she could have gotten at least a part-time position. Ideally, she would have picked one in which could have earned some money (representing a form of independence from men) and practiced a form of nurturing the weak (reinforcing her opinions of her own strengths). She might have taken a job as a teacher's aide, a day-care center employee, or an employee in a hospital, clinic, or nursing home. Millions of women, without even realizing it, make this very adjustment when their kids start school, but Monica must have balked at this kind of solution out of principle. It was, according to her survival plan, the man's duty to support the family, in exchange for such benefits as proper amounts of sexual release, hot meals, and all the TV he wanted.

Survival plans die hard. Making new ones takes courage and resolve. Yet it is only with such courage and resolve that life will change for us if love hurts. That decision is *ours:* the ogre hides within our homes, not outside.

It's Never Too Late

I have suggested that the Survival Plan comprises a set of "how-to's" for getting through life. Often people ask me: Can I write down my survival plan on a sheet of paper as if it were a shopping list? Can I draw it as if it were a diagram of my car's electrical system?

The answer to these questions is "NO." The survival plan is actually an unconscious pattern of living that all of us formulate from bits and pieces of wish-fulfillment starting in childhood and going on into adult life.

A young boy starts to piece together his plan for life around the age of four when he tries hard to win strong approval from his mother. He observes, quite correctly, that his father enjoys a good bit of attention from the mother, especially on days when the father works long hours. One of the little boy's first conclusions about surviving is that if he wishes to enjoy the warmth and loving of a woman and family, he must pursue some kind of meaningful work. A little later, when he becomes closer to his father, he may want to have a job just like his Dad's. As he's exposed to TV and outside influences, his choice of jobs may change. When he reaches adolescence and realizes that his

The Survial Plan

pleasures cost money, his survival plan may again be altered to give greater consideration to finances.

These are just a few of the many factors that go into the making of our blueprint for living. It is a complicated procedure, entailing a very delicate balancing act, and many things can go wrong.

Consider, for example, what kinds of impression the little boy would put into his survival plan if his father were desperately unhappy with his job and drank too much, if his mother weren't the kind of woman he wanted to get close to, if his outside influences vividly illustrated that crime pays well, if his mother cheated on his father when he spent those long hours at work, and so on. If these or other mishaps produced holes in the boy's survival plan, and if he were unable to repair them himself in later life, they would become his future spouse's responsibility. And if she proved unable to right the wrongs, she would suffer, too.

Thinking about the defects in this young man's survival plan prompts me to recall some of the later sessions in the treatment of Elizabeth, the patient discussed at such length in earlier chapters. By the time I have in mind, Elizabeth herself had improved so much that most of the discussion focused on her husband Mark.

It was clear that Mark was not adjusting to the changes in Elizabeth. The disputes at home were quieter than before, but much more serious. Elizabeth did not *need* Mark any more, and she really began to question her love for him.

"Things have really gone down the tubes at home" (her smile was imbued with a certain aloofness), "and, you know, I can't really even get upset about it."

I gave reassurance with a warning. "You know, if Mark adjusts to the change by changing himself, you'll both make it and have a good marriage. But if he keeps chugging along the way he's programmed now, your marriage is doomed."

"I know." Her matter-of-factness and bland unconcern—her

lack of terror—all attested to her change.

"**The root of all** these troubles is Mark's ambivalence. . ."

"Ambivalence?"

". . .opposite feelings like love and hate, for the same person at the same time."

"And I'm that person?"

"**I'm afraid you're only the tip of the iceberg.** The ambivalence is more or less ingrained in Mark's computer program on how he handles women."

"It doesn't take a Freud to see that Mark's relationship with his mother is what started all this, but it's clearly his fault for not ending it somewhere down the line."

Elizabeth became pensive. "I wish I could figure out what makes him tick. I mean, I finally lose weight and stop complaining and he's still not happy. Just what does he want?"

She really wanted an answer, but the edge of desperation was gone from her voice. I talked about Mark.

"Mark developed an inaccurate and unfair opinion of women from his mother during his childhood, and he simply hasn't let go of it since. Every woman fits into one or another of his categories: she's either an intimidating shrew who drives him to drink or a lustful siren who behaves like a whore. There's no middle ground; there's no individual judgment."

"Where did. . .I mean, how did he develop these two views?" (Elizabeth wondered what category she fell into.)

"Mark's dad was a drunk, and Mark believed his mother drove him to it. His mother was a forceful women, and this quality frightened Mark as a little boy. We learn gentleness and tenderness from our mothers, and Mark was so afraid of the woman, he simply never learned these things; that's why he seems so practical, so cold, and perhaps so unromantic at times. Mark viewed his father as a genuine victim at home, and probably with good reason. Do you remember the smoky room and the two strangers, A and B, in there?"

"Yes."

"Well, you'll remember that one of the strangers sat closer to you and this was okay because this person looked like you. This is the parent of the same sex. We inherit a lot of things from this person, some desirable and some not. As Mark incorporated more aspects of his father, he felt more like him, and as Mark felt more like his father, he felt more victimized by his mother. He also inherited a view of himself as weak and helpless. The combination is a bad one: a person who feels he is a victim but who feels helpless to fight back is a dangerous person to have a relationship with. It's like the short kid on the block who is always picked on by the bigger kids, and is constantly in fights not only trying to prove himself but trying to avenge all the unjust treatment associated with being a victim."

Elizabeth started to feel some sympathy for Mark. "Those are some tough beginnings."

"Yes, they are, and guess who most of his vengeance is directed at? Guess who victimized Mark first? And guess who Mark blames for *everything* that goes wrong in his life?"

"Me?" she asked.

"You and every woman who fits his notion of the female image. Mark blames his mother for his father's drinking, which is translated into Mark blames his mother for his father's weakness, which is translated into Mark blames his mother for his own weakness, which is translated into. . ."

I gestured toward Elizabeth.

". . .Mark blames Elizabeth for every single thing that goes wrong with his life."

I continued. "When you are a little heavy and look and dress matronly, or when you're under stress and try to erase your own weak feelings by mothering Mark, something clicks in Mark's unconscious mind: you unwittingly fall into that nasty parallel started by his mother so many years ago. That's when his ambivalence toward you—his feeling of love and hate—emerges. He loves you because you are nurturing him and thus erasing his feeling of being deprived of such nurturing in childhood, and he enjoys this for a while. But the feelings of warmth and nurturing he gets from you remind his unconscious of what he *didn't* get as a child and he gets angry. At this time, if you haven't stopped the nurturing, he provokes a fight which surely puts an end to it. He **is then able, legitimately in his mind, to express the anger inside** him. That's why your arguments are so inappropriately violent, and why your marriage is such a see-saw.."

Elizabeth wanted some answers about their sex life. We had talked somewhat about it in previous sessions and had briefly touched on it when we discussed Mark's relationship with his mother.

I brought the facts together for Elizabeth: "Mark's mother was such a coldly powerful woman that his budding feelings of sexuality were suppressed, and Mark very mechanically funneled them into what he thought were nasty little cubbyholes—forbidden areas of illicit desire inhabited by women who were made for just that. So sex was something to be had with sluts, and marrying was something to be engineered in order to get someone to serve as a good target for vengeance.

"Part of the woman's punishment takes the form of his being a very self-centered lover, one who has never learned the art of tenderness. And of course, when you look matronly, or are mothering him, feelings of incest well up in his not-so-unconscious mind, and he either has trouble getting the sex act started, or if he does get going, he wants to end it quickly, and usually does, far too soon for your needs. If he has had any extramarital affairs, I'm quite sure they were with women whom Mark considered sleazy.

"Since you've lost weight and have become more self-confident, Mark can no longer play-act you into a mother-figure, so you naturally fall into his only other category—the tramp. Since tramps by their very definition do not confine themselves to one man, Mark sees himself, when you are thin, as a man who cannot satisfy his woman, and this reinforces his weak image of himself as a replay of his weak, drunken father."

She thought for a minute and said, "It seems like no matter what I do, Mark has a problem with it."

"Not entirely true. You might notice that when you are fighting or when you lose weight, Mark becomes especially concerned about money and business."

"Yes, he has. He's been gone for hours on end."

I said, "Fathers are supposed to teach us the art of physical survival . . . earning a living to pay for food, clothing, and shelter. Since Mark's father left him feeling weak and helpless in the burning building that we talked about, Mark feels that in order to get out—to survive in life—he must do what his father didn't do: earn a good living. So earning money is Mark's best defense against the stress of daily living: every time he feels the world is down on him—just as his mother was always down on his father—Mark makes himself into the strong father he never had by chasing after the dollar."

Elizabeth filled in, " . . . there is nothing that Mark wants more in life than to be rich. Money is his god."

"Yes, Elizabeth, money is a primary goal for Mark because it is the only thing left in life that he believes will make him feel worthwhile enough to survive. Some men can do it by being Casanovas and one-night-stand lovers, but Mark has such a bad opinion of women that the sex act holds little significance for him except physical release; and because it is only relief, he finds little support for his virility in it."

She seemed brightened by all this discovery, and the solution seemed very simple to her.

"Why don't we get Mark in here, and just tell him all this?"

"I wish it were that simple, but it isn't. The answers to a lot of life's problems are very often right in front of our noses, and yet we blind ourselves to the obvious. If we just told this to Mark, he would think we were talking about someone else. Most of these interacting forces we have talked about are hidden from conscious awareness. On first hearing of them, we allow them to come out for few seconds, but then they are quickly pushed back into the closet of our unconscious mind. Also, Mark is in rather precarious balance right now, and to blast him with such a preposterous theory would be like chopping a hole in his lifeboat—his very last hope for survival.

She seemed concerned. "You mean, he'd go off the deep end?"

"No, his defenses would come to the rescue. He would immediately say out loud that we were both nuts, and he might even accuse you of an adulterous plot. A lot of women who are helped through either therapy or regular medical treatment face such accusations from their husbands; the wives' behavior reflects the gratitude felt towards the doctor-father figure, and the husband feels that his position as all-knowing healer is being usurped. This is especially true when the husband may be going through some stress and having trouble with his own self-assurance."

Elizabeth thought for a second. "That's why Mark doesn't bother me any more—I can look at his opinions as merely his point of view rather than statements pertaining to me."

"That's right. The better you feel about yourself, the less you need to worry about what Mark says and does. Your relationship, at least from your end, improves because you now *choose* to love Mark instead of *needing* to love him."

The Survival Plan

She was a bit saddened. "Is he so screwed up that he'll never change? I mean, if we can't tell him all this, how is he gonna know?"

I shocked her with the next statements. "I didn't say Mark was screwed up. I think he's perfectly normal."

"NORMAL?? You call all this normal?"

"It only looks screwed up because we've taken it all apart. When it's all put together, it runs fine. Mark still earns a living, he laughs every now and then, he functions. It's like a clock that runs, but doesn't keep good time. It looks fine at a glance, and we don't notice the time problem until we compare it to another clock. If we take it all apart and spread out the pieces, it looks like a hopeless mess. Some people do well when they get taken all apart, have a part or two fixed, and then get put back together. Some don't. I think Mark needs to be adjusted without taking him apart."

Elizabeth was very curious. "How do we do that?"

I wound the session to a close. "Mark has already started to repair his own clock without us. He's been seeing a lot of Walter lately, hasn't he?"

△   ▽   △

I smile now when I recall that conversation. A survival plan is a very delicate instrument, and tinkering with it can sometimes be a dangerous procedure. In this case, however, Walter's guileless presence worked a transformation. The magic worked slowly and subtly, but it worked.

Questions For Thought

1. *Do you see yourself as strong enough to provide most of your physical and emotional needs with little help from others?*

If your answer is an emphatic "no," then you probably have strong, perhaps excessive, dependency needs—tendencies to depend on others for help solving problems—and this situation makes your survival plan an important part of your loving. Loving may be more of a need than a want.

If your answer is "yes" or equivocal, then you probably have an established (not necessarily sound) survival plan to get through life.

2. *Do you remember your parents worrying about money a lot?*

If money was a frequent topic of family discussion, you may have incorporated this tendency to worry and now find yourself with a survival plan and love relationship centered on money.

3. *Were you the youngest child or an unexpected child?*

Sometimes these siblings place additional strain on the family budget and may hear words to that effect. Such words are incorporated into early attitudes about making it through life.

4. *Was your parent of the same sex basically happy with life?*

Again, incorporation plays a role here. If you had inadequate contact with this parent (or no recollection of any contact) then you may have trouble with a clear concept of what happy living is. If you had an unhappy parent of the same sex, then you may find yourself chronically depressed, or you may have formulated a survival plan directly opposite to your unhappy parent's.

5. *Are you in a love relationship where you feel that you are more committed than your lover? Do you love too fast, too hard?*

If you answered "yes" to either of these questions, this chapter is especially important for you. Your survival plan is not only the most important part of your loving, it may very well be the only part.

6. *Does your spouse or lover make more money than you do?*

This question may or may not have significance for you. Money often dictates power and lack of money implies dependency. For secure individuals whose survival plans are unimportant to them, who holds the power in a relationship is also unimportant. For

The Survival Plan

most people, the father-figure gives this security: if your father made a decent living and never worried too much about money, you probably find yourself not letting money influence your loving. You are a very lucky person.

For most, money and power in a relationship is almost always an issue. This is why "equal pay for equal work" is such an important point in Women's Rights—the very structure of a love relationship, sadly enough, is often affected by the size of a paycheck.

7. *If your marriage were to break up tomorrow, could you survive financially?*

This question is not only very important food for thought, it is a good indicator of how much your survival plan may mean to your loving.

8. *Are you the primary support for more than two people besides yourself?*

Money, out of situational necessity, is important to you. If you are divorced or widowed and have children, then finances surely play a role in keeping your survival plan alive, and you may thus act accordingly in a love relationship.

9. *Are you divorced, paying alimony or child support?*

In this situation, you have the responsibility of keeping a survival plan alive with none of the advantages of being a parent (or at least far fewer than normal). The bitterness that develops from long-term support payments surely will affect not only future relationships, but how you view loving in general.

10. *Do you believe in UFO's, occult supernatural forces or miracles?*

When life is difficult and survival plans seem to be failing, a need develops to believe in extra-natural forces that communicate with us—perhaps even help us in some benevolent way.

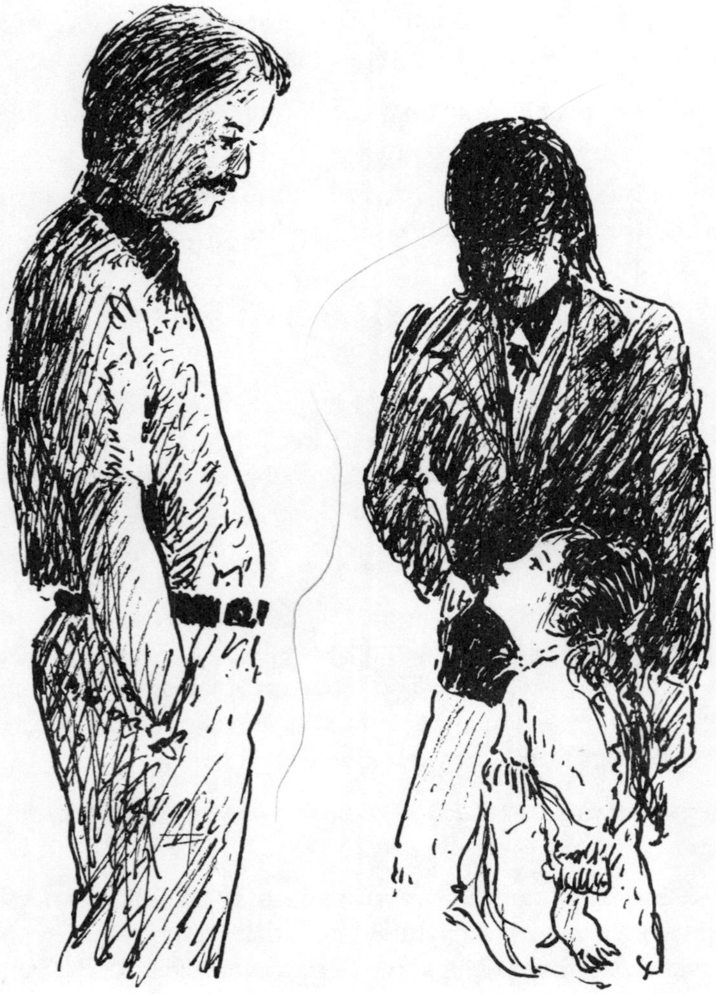

CHAPTER 12

The Love Debt

Victims and Bad Guys

The love debt is a legacy we inherit from our parents or parent-figures, and it is a bequest we receive within their own lifetime. It establishes our view of the parental relationship as an imbalance in need of rectifying. One parent is perceived as the "good guy" or victim, and one parent as the "bad guy" or person to be feared. If we take our perceptions of "good guys" and "bad guys" too seriously, we are likely to bring many unconscious and unhealthy preconceptions to our adult love relationships.

I must stress the word "perceive." The objective truth about how our parents interrelated means little to us in this context. What matters is *how we saw them* interact.

The "good guy" in our parenting relationship might be described in any one or more of the following ways: a victim; whom we see as somehow coming up with the short end of the stick in the power structure and decision-making process; a parent who has been abandoned or sent away; a parent who who has been physically hurt by the other parent; a parent who complains a lot in front of the family about how unhappy he or she is; a parent who is an alcoholic or who commits suicide. It doesn't matter if the victim-parent was a good or bad parent to you, or even if you liked or disliked the parent. All that matters is how you saw your parents in their relationship to each other.

Let's look at some examples: An alcoholic father who is henpecked by a nagging wife will be seen as a victim by his children. An absent father in a divorced family will be seen as a victim if the children perceive the mother as being difficult and hard to live with. A woman who is beaten up by her husband in front of her children will be perceived as a victim.

The "bad guy" in our parenting relationship might be described in any one or more of these ways: the parent whom we see as making most of the decisions, right or wrong, in our family; the physically abusive parent; the absent parent in a divorce situation whom we perceive as having left to seek his or her own pleasure; the parent who is most closely involved with our criticism and discipline. A little girl can be very close to her Daddy, and be the "apple of his eye," but still view him as the "bad guy" in her version of the parents' relationship.

After each of us has established in our own mind which parent is the victim and which the villain, the love debt may emerge in one of two ways. The first (and the more common) is the situation in which you perceive the parent of the same sex as the "bad guy" and the parent of the opposite sex as the victim, we call this the ROMANTIC TYPE of love debt. The second type is, of course, the opposite—we see the parent of the opposite sex the "bad guy" and the parent of the opposite sex as the victim; and we call this the PRACTICAL TYPE of love debt. The logic behind these names will soon be clear.

To understand how and why we act the way we do in paying off these love debts later in life, we need to understand the relationship of each of our parents to ourselves. When we talk about our relationship to the parent of the same sex, we use the term *incorporation*. Incorporation is the unconscious process of a child's selecting certain traits from the

The Love Debt

parent of the same sex and using these traits in the child's own growing personality. The more exposure we have to this parent of the same sex, the more traits we incorporate. The more desirable traits are more readily assimilated; the characteristics we don't like are absorbed, but as we grow older and realize our distaste for these traits, we push them back into our unconscious behavior patterns.

As a growing boy, you may have incorporated your father's fine qualities of strength and love for the work ethic, and you may demonstrate these traits by being a successful leader in business. You may have also picked up his dislike of animals, and realizing later in life that you don't really like this trait, you may find yourself behaving *reactively* by having several dogs. Every time you dote on and spoil the dogs, you are, in effect, repressing your father's legacy of disliking animals.

How important the love debt is in your life is very closely linked with how much incorporation you experienced as a child. Let us suppose that you are the romantic type of debtor who saw your father as the "bad guy" and your mother as the "victim." The more exposure you had to your father, the more of his "bad guy" traits you will perceive yourself as having picked up. If you indeed had such closeness to him, then you also perceive yourself as a "bad guy" with a grave responsibility to repay the opposite sex for all the wrongs done.

Other circumstances can intensify the love debt. The young girl whose father left because of a divorce may be the romantic type of debtor if she perceives her mother as having caused his leaving. If she has had a lot of exposure to her mother, as most girls have, she may incorporate the blame for her father's leaving, and feel responsible for it. Later in life, in her love relationships, her love debt may be intensified because she may feel not only that the injustice against her father must be erased, but she may also fear for her own survival, thinking she will drive away her husband or lover, just as she "drove away" her father. In order to avert this, she becomes an obsessed approval seeker. This is behavior typical of the romantic type of debtor, as we are about to see.

If we are heterosexual, we don't normally incorporate a lot of indentity traits from our parent of the opposite sex, but we do form opinions about this parent. If, for example, we dislike what we perceive, we will carry this opinion forward into our own adult relationships. And we may maintain our views stubbornly even when confronted with powerful evidence to the contrary.

I remember once visiting a local gun club where several men were sitting around watching TV. An advocate of the women's movement was speaking on the screen, and the discussion in the room quickly heated up as the various men expressed their views on "women's lib." The fracas ended with a full can of beer being thrown at the TV. Fortunately the guns were outside, safely stowed on a gun rack.

These men obviously saw their fathers as strong, macho "bad guys" and their mothers as weak and victimized. Seeing a vivid portrayal of the opposite power structure made their love debts seem foolish, thus potentially undermining their entire approach to women. Rather than reassess their preconceptions, they threw beer at the TV.

In the same vein, a young girl who sees her father as an ominous figure will carry that opinion forward, and deal with all men as if they were ogres. She will view with suspicion and even shun men who seem gentle and reserved.

Just what kind of relationships develop with each of the two types of love debts? The romantic type of debtor, who sees the parent of the same sex as "bad guy" and the parent of the opposite sex as victim, tends to take a lot of blame for what goes wrong in relationships personally, and looks to repay the victim. The romantic debtor may display one or more of the following traits: silent-suffering martyrdom; approval-seeking that falls apart if the lover is angry or upset; insistence on being the "giver" in a love relationship; wanting a happy ending in all love stories; loving very hard and intensely; and (perhaps) getting along better with the opposite sex than with friends of the same sex.

The practical type of debtor, who sees the parent of the same sex as a victim and the opposite sex as a villain, has an entirely different attitude toward loving—and usually is totally unaware of it. Since this person perceives the parent of the same sex as a victim, he or she usually incorporates sufficiently to see himself or herself as a victim, too. For such

The Love Debt

a person loving takes on many aspects of vengeance. In relationships this person may seem practical, superficial, and even cold. Typical behavior patterns include: speaking up when something hurts; seeking to have every action in the relationship benefit him or her in some way; being practical and unemotional; having multiple relationships, one after another, with relatively little depth of feeling; and (perhaps) having many good, strong peer relationships with the same sex.

Can the two kinds of love debts overlap? Can we be both a romantic and practical love debtor? Yes, indeed we can. It depends on how we perceive shifts in our parents' relationship. It may also depend on whether we have the occasion to interact with others whose behavior blatantly contradicts our own preconceptions—and on whether we are able to recognize and accept the contradiction. When this shifting of perceptions takes place, there can be trouble in an otherwise stable relationship.

Carol, one of the women on my office staff, demonstrated this pattern very well. She had not seen her father for thirty-five years, and because her memories of him were filtered through her mother's eyes, she saw him as a bad guy—a man who had deserted his family to gratify his own desires. So she herself married a "bad guy" in hope of both extracting love from him and paying back the "debt" of her father's desertion.

Carol, in essence, needed to dislike her husband. When he was pleasant and kind to her, it made her feel terribly guilty for all the abuse she had directed toward him, and this anger at herself caused severe ulcer disease and depression. Her behavior easily showed her husband that she didn't do well when he was sweet and kind, so he went back to being his old, demanding self.

The critical problem arose when she met her father again after 35 years, and realized he was a sweet, kind man and that her mother had lied to her. Whenever she visited with her father, she unconsciously became aware that her marriage to a "bad guy" was a mistake, and the specter of divorce tormented her. Divorce was not in her survival plan, because her mother had been divorced three times and this instability had brought nothing but misery to the family, so she solved the conflict by not seeing her real father any more. As often as she could see her husband as a "bad guy" (and she provoked most of his hurtful behavior), she could feel justified in extracting vengeance and thus paying back the love debt she had inherited from her parents.

As Carol's story demonstrates, keeping our survival plan intact takes precedence over repaying the love debt. Keeping body and soul intact, food on the table, and a roof over our heads is far more important to us than correcting the injustices we saw in childhood. In the final analysis, it's our parents' problem, not ours. Our need to see ourselves as having had a balanced childhood is not as strong as our need to survive, and thus our payment of the love debt is an inclination rather than an obsession.

Why We Just Can't Say Goodbye

We've all experienced it ourselves or heard of it from others: that horrible feeling of being trapped by guilt in a bad relationship. There may be many reasons why we are trapped, but the need to repay a love debt is probably the most common.

I remember Anna, a woman of about twenty-six, who came to therapy solely for the purpose of getting enough courage and support to get out of her marriage.

I asked her what was keeping her from just walking out the door. Was it money?

"No, I make plenty of money, and besides I could always go back and stay with my parents until I got on my feet if I had to. It's just guilt. Every time I go to leave, Michael practically gets on his hands and knees and begs me not to go . . . when he cries, it just kills me." She was very definite about her intention to get out of the marriage, but couldn't really put her finger on what the problem was.

"Michael just doesn't make me happy any more. I don't understand it. He's being very good to me now. . .maybe I can't ever be happy."

Anna went on to tell me that her husband had made most of the money that now accounted for their pleasant lifestyle. In the earlier years of their relationship, he hadn't been so kind and considerate. He had felt that since he made the money, he had the privilege of being nasty whenever he felt the urge. He had stayed out late whenever he pleased, and had complained constantly about her spending money, even for necessities.

In spite of its one-sidedness, the marriage (in its fourth year) had a strange stability to it. Yet it was plain to Anna that she didn't feel any real peace or contentment.

On her twenty-sixth birthday, Anna must have felt as though her whole life was going to be like this. She panicked and asked for a divorce. She and Michael separated for a while, but as soon as he started to call her and cry over the phone, she went back. She said she was fine as long as Michael didn't call.

While she was gone, Michael had asked her what there was about himself that he could change to make her happier, and she had told him that the marriage needed to be on more equal terms and that he needed to be kinder and more considerate. After all, this was what every marriage was based on, wasn't it? So when she returned home, Michael changed completely. He did most of the housework, took extra time with their daughter, and treated Anna with utmost courtesy and respect. In spite of his changes, she was more miserable than ever, a victim of her own feelings of guilt.

She realized that she didn't want him even though he had carried out her every wish for change, and this confused her. She started to realize that she didn't know what she wanted out of life. To add to her confusion the men she dated while she was separated were handsome, witty, charming, rich, and good lovers, but every one had bored her after two or three dates.

Every time Michael was nice to her after she moved back, she felt guilty because of her lack of feeling for him. Trapped by her own guilt in a relationship she didn't understand, she soon began to project the blame for her entrapment onto Michael.

"He's only being nice to get me to stay. As soon as he knows I'm staying, he'll go back to his old ways."

I deflated her projection with a very real possibility. "Anna, suppose Michael stays nice for four more years?"

She became flustered. "Oh, I don't know. I can't take it anymore. I just want to be alone."

Without realizing it, she was admitting there was a conflict within herself, and this conflict really had little to do with Michael. Her desire to be alone was simply a wish to escape the horns of a dilemma, and that dilemma was a love debt Anna had been saddled with as a kid.

"Anna, you don't feel good when you're living with Michael, and you don't feel good when you're not living with Michael. Maybe Michael doesn't have anything to do with how you feel at all?"

"That's ridiculous."

"Perhaps, it is, but you've got to admit there appears to be something deeper going on here. The problem you're having is not with any particular man, because the number-one man has changed his ways several times to please you and that didn't work. You even changed men several times, and that didn't make you feel good either. So it's not any individual man or what he does or doesn't do or what he has or doesn't have that makes you feel bad. It's the interrelating that gives you your bad feelings. Relationships with the opposite sex make you feel bad, because they carry certain responsibilities with them."

"Does that mean I'm irresponsible and will never be happy with one man?"

"No, Anna, it means that your love relationships have burdens attached to them that many people don't have, or don't care about."

I got her to talk about her parents in order to bring the love debt out into the open. Her mother was a very forceful, domineering woman who had divorced and reconciled with

The Love Debt

Anna's father twice, and was now on the verge of another divorce from him. Anna's allegiance towards her father was enhanced by the fact that she thought her mother really didn't like her very much. Anna felt that her mother showed preference to her older brother and two younger sisters. She didn't realize that her mother may have been hard on her because of her warm, close relationship with the victimized father. Which feeling had come first was hard to say.

This was Anna's love debt: to find a man who could stand up to the selfishness and abuse that Anna felt her mother had inflicted on her father. The love debt was intensified by Anna's relationship with her mother. The mother had told Anna repeatedly that she was never going to succeed at anything in life because she could never do anything right. This type of rejection seriously undermined Anna's survival plan. Anna was thus damned to a life of repaying the love debt *in order to prove her mother wrong*.

The plot was set. Anna was a romantic type of love debtor who clearly saw her parent of the same sex as a "bad guy" and her parent of the opposite sex as a victim. On top of this, her mother had left her with a very poor image of herself, thus giving Anna a very shaky survival plan. Since Anna did not like most of the things her mother told her, she had sought refuge and solace in her father. She had carried this preference forward into her adult love relationships and thus, her love debt had been born: she had to find a male who could be a suitable father-figure, and yet be strong enough (unlike her father) to prove that women were wrong much of the time. This would give Anna her much-needed feelings of being worthwhile and able to survive.

Michael played his part admirably. Every time he pushed his weight around in the marriage, he was, in effect, showing Anna that the woman in a relationship didn't have much of a chance to be a bully. This behavior suggested to Anna that her mother wasn't the tough guy she acted like, and that her predictions of failure for Anna were probably meaningless. This is what kept the marriage somewhat stable, although uncomfortable, for the first four years.

Unfortunately, Anna did not like her mother's domineering and irascible nature (because the fury was often directed at her), and thus did not incorporate these emotional plates of armor from her mother. Anna just couldn't breathe fire the way her mother could. She was sensitive, and got tired of the constant power abuse by Michael. Sure, it was great unconsciously to "watch" her mother's predictions about living and loving get torn apart; but after four years it was starting to hurt. Besides, she was beginning to hear good things about herself from the outside world, from other men and women who didn't act in this little play, and she simply no longer needed Michael to disprove her mother's prophecy of doom. She finally got tired of a marriage based on one-sided emotional put-downs directed at her. Her marriage had suffered, but it had allowed her to pay off her love debt, so she didn't need Michael any more.

Why, then, was there the problem of "saying goodbye"? Why did she feel so unusually guilty about leaving Michael? Any why did no other man seem to make her happy beyond the third date?

If Michael had kept up his macho-type behavior after Anna came home, there would have been no chance of permanent reconciliation; Anna was tired of it, and she had been fine during the separation. But Michael must have had love debts of his own that we haven't considered here, because he realized how much he needed Anna as soon as she left. His forcefulness and dominance, which had served their purpose so well in paying off Anna's romantic-type love debt, were now driving away someone he loved and probably needed as well. In order to save his marriage, he changed, and he changed into the kind of man Anna thought healthy marriages needed: sweet, gentle, kind and considerate.

Michael, however, carried the reversal too far when he began cleaning house, cooking meals, and playing nursemaid far beyond his share of such duties. The answer to why it was so hard to say good-bye was that Anna's desertion, and Michael's pleading and manipulating to get her back home, were living replays of Anna's mother and father going through their own up-and-down love relationship. Anna could not desert her weak, victimized "father."

The plot was being replayed so perfectly that I was curious to see how closely the second set of actors resembled the first. I asked Anna to bring in a photo album. When she did, I looked through it and selected four pictures of faces very close to the same size. They were photographs of Anna, Michael, and Anna's father and mother. I studied the pictures for a few minutes, and then made some notes. I told Anna to hold the pictures of Michael and her father side by side and answer some questions.

"Anna, you have pictures of two men in front of you. Could you say that they both have a full head of hair with the same hairline, even though Michael's hair is black and your father's is gray?"

She began to smile, not at the similarity I was hoping she'd see, but at the silliness of it. "Yes, I'll give you that one."

"Okay. Now look at how tall they are. Could you say that they are within one inch of being the same height?" I was smiling now.

She giggled. "All right, they're both exactly five-eight."

"Would you say that both men have stocky builds with upper torsos larger than their lower bodies?"

She was smiling knowingly now, beginning to accept the love-debt idea. "Both my father and Michael have such skinny legs, and the men I dated all had muscular legs."

We went on like that through four or five other physical traits that were very similar. I then took the photos and covered the faces with some onionskin tracing paper. I made outlines of the jawlines, lower lips, and hairlines. I showed Anna the tracings and asked if she could pick out Michael or her father. She couldn't. I gave back the photos and asked if she could pick out Michael's tracing using the photographs. She couldn't: both tracings fit both photographs almost perfectly.

She laughed aloud, and seemed pleased that we had solved the great mystery. "So I married somebody like my father—doesn't everybody?"

"Some people do marry a person similar to their parent of the opposite sex. If the child had a good relationship with that parent, I think it's a good choice. But people with a serious love debt to pay very often marry a physical replica, at least once, anyway, to make the play seem more real. If they're going to have affairs behind the back of the physically similar spouse, they'll do it with someone of totally opposite physical appearance. By the way, what did those fellows that you dated look like, the ones you found so boring?"

She was laughing and continued to laugh as she walked out of the office. "They were tall, blond, all over six-two, with slender builds and thinning hair . . . the exact opposite of Michael, and my father, I guess."

She made her next appointment and was leaving. I stopped her quietly and brought up a point we had completely neglected to mention. "The sex is better when the unconscious mind isn't screaming 'incest' in your ear, isn't it?" She smiled as she waved goodbye.

After several sessions of insight-reinforcement, I told Anna to do nothing for six months to a year. Live peacefully with Michael and let things take their natural course. I did place her in a volunteer situation one day a week in a nursing home in order to completely dispel her ideas about herself being an unaffectionate, ungiving person like her mother. The less she saw herself as being like her mother, the less Michael's pleading and begging would remind her of her father. Time is a great healer, and as Anna got more and more involved in the nurturing and caring projects, her image of herself improved and strengthened tremendously. Michael's moods and unhealthy needs affected Anna less and less;

it was up to Michael whether he wanted to continue to play out his own love debt (perhaps getting another leading actress) or let his love debt die also and begin to sow the seeds of healthier love with Anna.

Paying off the Love Debt

It is important after all, to realize that the love debt need not hold us in shackles throughout our lives, following us from relationship to relationship. For most of us, the love debt can fade and even disappear through three processes of living: maturing, forming a serious love commitment, and becoming actively involved in nurturing.

The love debt is like a wound to our sense of self. Like any wound it heals with the elixir of time. As we mature and accrue successes and failures, we realize that adult living is full of triumphs and mistakes. We also come to realize that our parents, the creators of our sense of injustice about love, were people who had their own share of wins and losses, virtues and imperfections.

Most of us have had acquaintances who had been married for twenty or so years with no apparent problems, when suddenly one of the spouses just up and left. One instance I'm thinking of involved a forty-four-year-old man with nearly grown children who left home and took up residence with a twenty-two-year-old. Friends were mystified: the new lover had none of the beauty, charm, and wit of the man's wife, but he was persistent in saying: "At last, I know what love is." His love debt must have faded away through the years of marriage, and both husband and wife must have been too busy to nurture the healthier aspects of their loving. When this man no longer felt it necessary to pay for the sins of his father against his mother, he found someone he wanted rather than needed.

This disruption of lives underscores the importance of not only developing healthy loving and sharing in marriage, but of keeping the debt in its proper, *minor* perspective. The love debt is merely a tendency to act a certain way in marriage, unless you allow it to become the entire basis for your mate selection and marital fulfillment. Simply waiting for time to redeem the love debt can be a hazardous course. It is far better to be aware of it and try actively to diminish it.

If you keep the love debt in its proper perspective, you can also marry it away. The problem can be resolved in marriage if your spouse interacts with you so as to work through the injustice.

Suppose a man had an alcoholic for a mother and watched his father and the family suffer the expected neglect from such behavior. If he reacts violently every time his wife has a glass of wine or she doesn't have dinner on the table at 5:30, he is letting the love debt get out of perspective. But if he is aware of his mistrust of women's strengths, he may take an effort to be especially supportive of his wife, so that each time she succeeds in a project and achieves a measure of personal gratification, it will be a victory for both of them.

After struggling through all of this intricate theory about loving, it may seem anticlimactic to say that the love debt can be paid off completely and easily. The way to do this, of course, is the topic of the whole book: nurturing and caring behavior as a therapeutic approach to feeling better and living a more fulfilled life.

Just how does nurturing and caring behavior pay off the love debt for you? It does its work by making life seem balanced and worthwhile. You feel worthy of enjoying life's pleasure because you have shown yourself to be a decent, caring person. The need to "make right" is done away with and replaced by the impulse to "do right."

If you are the romantic type of debtor who feels you are the "bad guy" causing pain to members of the opposite sex, practicing nurturing and caring erases the unpleasant traits incorporated from your parent of the same sex. A young man who takes time from a busy schedule to read French to a blind student will find it hard to continue viewing himself as a "bad guy." His unconscious memories of his domineering and unaffectionate father—traits with which he sometimes identifies—are dimished whenever he experiences the warmth and gratitude of the blind student. The effects of such erasure linger. With the love debt thus "paid off," he no longer needs to play the approval-seeker, atoning for the past, but instead can begin to love others for the joy that love can bring here and now.

The practical type of debtor can also pay off the love debt with nurturing and caring behavior. The competitive edge, the vengefulness and power-seeking disposition of such a person arise from the feeling of having been "done wrong." A young man whose father suffered at the hands of his mother will take those notions of suffering unto himself and carry them forward into later life. He will have a weak image of himself, not only because strength was not one of the virtues passed on from his father, but because the young man sees himself as a victim. Just like the short kid on the block who thinks everyboby is picking on him, he will deal with the world by hitting first and talking later.

Not unexpectedly, this fellow's love life will be a shambles. Yet if he were to commit one hour a week to the Special Olympics, it isn't likely he could keep his idea that *he* is a victim for very long. Not only would he do away with his feelings of victimization, and thus give up his drive for vengeance and competition in his love relationships, but he would quickly develop a view of himself as strong and worthwhile. (He would also be helping some pretty deserving kids.)

△ ▽ △

The love debt, that legacy of injustice left you by your parents that damns you to a life of illogical attraction and unhealthy love for people who are only bound to hurt you, is an obsession for some and a minor inconvenience for others. Many people just wait until time diminishes the importance of the love debt. Some marry it away and hope nothing happens to upset the delicate balance. A few lucky ones learn that you can erase the debt with nurturing and caring. If you are able in this way to heal yourself, love will stop being a debt incurred by an insensitive parent's sin and become a gift of the soul for another human being.

Questions For Thought

1. *Do you perceive one of your parents as "stronger" than the other?*

In most instances, we perceive one parent as stronger than the other. This is what sets up a love debt. The love debt becomes more intense if we also perceive the weaker parent as a "victim" of sorts.

2. *Did you ever see or hear about one of your parents physically hurting the other? Was one parent afraid of the other?*

If your answer to these questions is "yes," your love debt may have significant intensity to affect the way you act in your love relationship—you may be an approval-seeker if the victim was your parent of the opposite sex or you may be chronically angry at the opposite sex if the victim was your parent of the same sex. The diagram on page 168 will help you to understand this a bit better.

3. *Did you find one parent easier to talk to . . . one you always asked things of?*

Even though this parent may not have suffered at the hands of the other parent, we have labeled this more gentle parent the "victim" or "good guy." For most romantic individuals this parent is the one of the opposite sex and for most practical types, it is the parent of the same sex.

4. *Before you were 17, did you lose one of your parents to death, divorce or desertion?*

The parent on whom you place the blame for the loss may very well be the "bad guy" in your love debt.

5. *If you lost a parent to death, do you "blame" that parent for leaving you?*

The normal grieving process has some "blame" or suppressed anger at the lost loved one, but when it doesn't get resolved and is carried into later life, it may surface in love relationships.

The Survival Plan

6. *If you had a parent leave home because of divorce or desertion, do you feel deep inside that it might have been your other parent's fault?*

Again, this question will help you decide who might be the "bad guy" or "good guy" in your love debt.

7. *Is your love relationship based on need rather than want? Is it hard to say "good-bye"?*

This is a difficult question to analyze precisely because everyone feels some need in loving and it is rarely easy to say "good-bye" to someone you may have shared a good part of your life with. If you can answer the question "yes" for many of the relationships, even superficial ones, it's a good bet that you are carrying a significant love debt, and you will not lose these feelings, which can make a love relationship a nightmare at times, until you "pay off" the love debt.

8. *Do you sometimes feel sorry for the opposite sex? Do you find that you can relate to them more easily than the members of your own sex? Do you try to please members of the opposite sex more than you think you should?*

"Yes" answers to these questions indicate that you are a romantic type of love debtor—a good lover, but easily hurt.

9. *Do you feel that your parent of the same sex got the "short end of the stick?"*

If you answer "yes" to this question, you are probably a practical type of love debtor, as the diagram in this chapter shows. You are more stable as a lover, and certainly more practical, but tend to be more self-serving and less sensitive than the romantic type.

10. *Are you angry at either or both of your parents?*

This is a very complex question that can best be handled by saying that if you are angry at your parent of the same sex, you will tend to redirect that anger at yourself. This will make you chronically depressed, self-destructive, or an approval seeker. And, you will be a romantic type of love debtor.

If you are angry at the parent of the opposite sex, you may transfer that anger to other people in later life, and not necessarily just the opposite sex. You are a practical type of love debtor.

11. *Do you think that you and your spouse have left a love debt to your own children? Can you undo it?*

It is difficult not to leave a love debt. The effects, however, can be minimized by keeping your marriage an equal sharing of power, decisions, and kind and gentle contact with your children. The discipline and criticism should certainly not be left to one parent. *Any* criticism should be appropriate and balanced with an equal amount of praise.

As long as your children live at home, you can undo the bad effects of a love debt.

CHAPTER 13

The Romantic Ideal

This is as good a place as any, I think, to stop and rest. Like travelers on a wearying journey, we need to camp on the side of a hill and look back at the road we've traveled and look forward to where we're going. This pause will help bring into focus what this book is about. Indeed, changing the pace here seems important because I still have a great deal to say to readers who have no great love debt and no serious defect in survival plan—yet still find love hurtful.

I have written this section on romantic expectations for people whose parents gave them enough of a sense of self-worth to be confident about surviving through life, and also successfully kept hidden from their offspring the strife in married life that creates the love debt. For these people, the weak link is the third supporting pillar beneath love relationships, the romantic ideal. Either they expect too much from love, or they are victims of a spouse or lover who does.

At this point we require a brief digression.

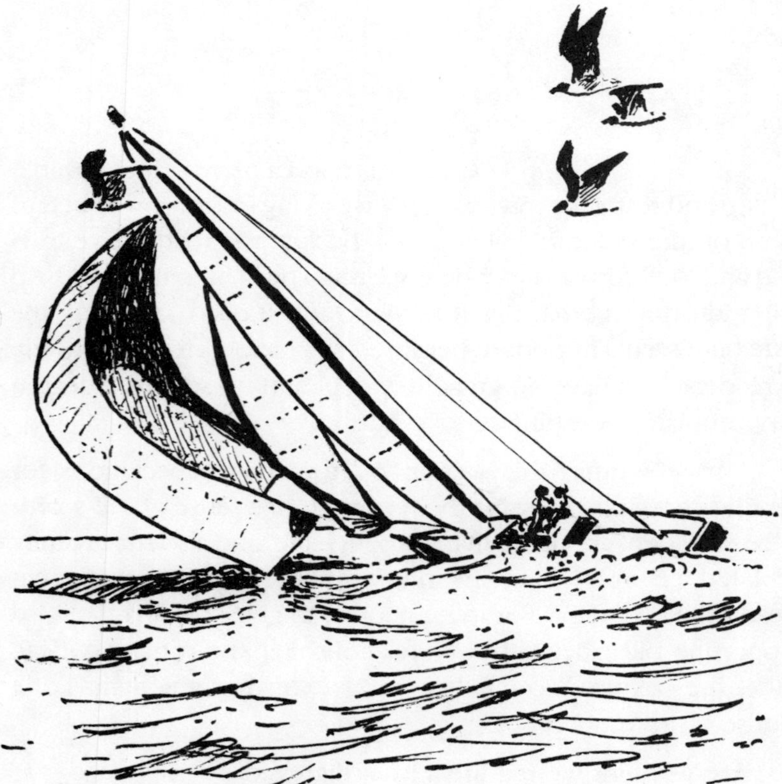

The Dark Ages, Kurt Vonnegut says, still haunt us. From those times, centuries ago, when the demons of the human personality were allowed to roam free and wreak havoc on families and clans trying to survive has come a pervasive fear about living. Those demons still lurk about, occasionally surfacing in the predator-like behavior of our criminals and sociopaths. So the fear has stayed with us throughout the ages, and sometimes it gets worse when a lot of demons surface together as they have during our wars.

To quiet this fear, the human intellect has, throughout the ages, invented things to make life seem easier and to distract us from our concerns about demons. Developing technology occasionally gives us things to make life seem better; sometimes it inadvertently gives the demons new toys to play with.

But technology began to come of age, so to speak, in the middle of the seventeenth century with the Industrial Revolution. In the last three-hundred years, we have been showered with gifts of machinery. These gifts have made life soft by comparison with the Old, Dark Days, and life in much of the world has surely become more orderly and civilized.

Today, when the demon of violent, predator-like behavior emerges in our lives, it seems a horrid aberration, a canker on our soft, sensitive skin. We begin to abhor this dark side of ourselves as if it were a stranger—a separate person.

In this sense, our benefactor has done us a disservice. Like little children we have been spoiled by the inventions of science and have come progressively to shun any kind of discomfort whatsoever. Now we no longer fear for our survival so much as we fear discomfort.

If the electric power is off for thiry minutes or so, we feel an uneasy annoyance. Indeed, we have come to feel that we are entitled to a burst of light when we turn on a switch. After all, we have become accustomed to having what we want. Unfortunately, we have come to view love in the same way.

Prior to the advent of "easy" living deriving from the Industrial Revolution, marriage was, in most cases, a practical arrangement. It begat children to farm the land; it brought money to some; it provided the opportunity for liturgically sanctioned sensual indulgence. What it lacked, however, was charm, warmth, mystery.

In the past 150 years, during which the drudgery of life has been alleviated for all but the most downtrodden classes, there has been more time to discover love as an entity in itself. The Romantics glorified it as a mystical experience. More "realistic" or "naturalistic" writers viewed love as a narcotic to numb the pain of life.

These views have been carried forward into our century, and magnified countless times by the movies and television. The hours and hours we spend absorbing these illusions trick us into believing that love is always available, and that it will always make us feel good.

Our hopelessly optimistic views about loving come from the media in many forms, but the three most egregious are magazine advertisements, television commercials, and live filmed dramas.

Magazine ads give us visual images of what people are "supposed" to look like. The message is subliminal, making us believe if we buy a certain product, love will be just around the corner in the form of a sloe-eyed beauty or a handsome prince in a Lamborghini. Television commercials tell us the same thing, but with movement and sound added, so that the message is even more vivid.

The message is that whatever love problem we have, we can solve it by simply using a certain product or service. If we feel lonely and unloved, perhaps we need to change dandruff shampoos. Now most of us really don't believe that part of the message, no matter how many times we see it. The association does, however, sell shampoo. In doing so, it leaves us with a very dangerous subliminal assumption: we tend to believe that we can *easily* get a warm and enthusiastic response from the opposite sex. Since these commercials are usually thirty-second spots, we absorb the short time-span also: we *expect* love to be good to us, and we expect it *fast*.

A lot of movies and television shows are especially harmful because they not only convince us that all love's problems and injustices can be easily solved, but they do it for us with characters that may replay some of our own love problems. This is precisely the idea, of course. There is a "bad guy" and a "good guy," just as at home, and the story line always has the "bad guy" make the "good guy" suffer numerous injustices, until the end when the "bad guy" gets his comeuppance. The longer the abuse by the "bad guy" is drawn out, the more eagerly awaited and gratifying is the resolution when justice is finally achieved.

We are, in essence, watching a created version of our love debt which always ends up repaid. This is not so bad in itself, but many times we mimic the behaviors of the people we identify with in the stories and then *expect* the same response from our spouse or lover.

It is an easily observed phenomenon. Men, controlling, manipulative like the characters so often seen on popular evening soap operas, who have cold, ruthless, mother figures, predictably spend their lives paying women back.

Men who have had critical, domineering fathers often enjoy seeing their fantasy strength come to life in the so-called splatter movies. "Dirty Harry" has not only gotten rid of a lot of "bad guys," but has paid back the love debt with a rather obvious symbol of maleness and potency—the .44 magnum.

Our heavy diet fo this stuff makes us somehow believe it, probably without even being aware that we do. We *expect* love always to match us with fantastically attractive, warm, sensitive lovers. We *expect* our electronic fantasies to always come true. All this expectation, all this unconscious assumption that love always travels a smooth path and never hurts, erodes our inborn ability to adapt.

Adaptation is the key to the resiliency of living, and certainly of loving. The gifts of technology have made our adapting skills less important, and as each new invention has come forth, we have become less proficient at adapting to discomfort. This rigidity may well damage our love relationships, as we become less and less capable of adjusting when loving disappoints us.

Because our fantasies about loving are so ingrained, irritable spouses, crying babies, and noisy kids seem intolerable at times. The more electronic fantasy we are exposed to, the more intolerable real life becomes. Instead of swallowing your pride and asking your spouse why he or she is in a bad mood, instead of accepting the fact that babies do cry, and instead of enduring the discomfort of effective parenting, you become paralyzed with disappointment and begin to feel shortchanged because, you think, this just isn't the way loving should be. In unconscious disgust, you turn to more escapist fantasy and watch TV. or commitment. Bob, who was just one of her current paramours, was

Such electronic daydreaming conditions your unconscious minds to think along the lines of a kind of fantasy whereby you can "work through" your wish-fulfillments. I'm referring to the totally unconscious "casting" of people around us into roles which play out the plots of our wish-fulfillment.

If you have a perfectly acceptable survival plan, and don't feel that you have a great love debt to repay, you may still use this type of play-acting to fulfill some of your expectations of the romantic ideal. This is not always unhealthy behavior. Yet, more often than not, unconsciously "using" people to chase after unrealistic romantic pleasures leads to hurtful relationships, loving that only appears to be real, and numerous, very painful breakups and reconciliations. This is a merry-go-round on which many of us find ourselves.

Let me tell you another story.

The Romantic

I didn't know Andrea through therapy; such people rarely seek counseling. She was intermittently breaking the heart of a friend of mine who would cruise by my house to catch me mowing the lawn and stop me for some free curbside counseling. He never got out of his car, as if to reassure me his stop would be only a momentary hello, but forty-five minutes later he would drive off, leaving me with a stiff lower back and a distinct lack of desire to finish the lawn.

She must have had something magical, because Bob convinced himself this was, at last, real love.

"Nunc scio quid sit amor," he would say, *"nunc scio quid sit amor."* And I would always have to ask what that meant, and he would raise his eyes and shake his head.

"I thought doctors knew Latin . . . it means, 'now I know what love is'."

Knowing Latin makes people sound impressive, I guess, and forty-four-year-old successful lawyers like to sound impressive. Yet in the last six months my friend Bob had started to act very peculiarly. He had convinced himself that, since this was at last real love, he should pursue it with great vigor, and he had walked out on a twenty-year marriage, leaving his wife and four sons.

All Bob's friends were frankly puzzled. He had seemed an ideally happy man. He had enjoyed his work, had had money in the bank, had played harder than the rest of us, and had really seemed to get along very well with his wife. She was attractive enough to hold the attention of any man at parties, and was to boot a very successful program director at a local television station. They had had no business splitting up.

He was chasing the romantic ideal, of course, but the woman he was chasing it with could not have been a worse choice. She had, to put it euphemistically, been around. Now I never got to know Andrea well, and I certainly have no wish to judge her unfairly. What I do know for certain is that she inflicted gratuitous pain on more than one man and that she herself always landed on her feet.

The men Andrea pursued seemed to be chosen for two traits: they had to be married, and they had to be rich. The fact that they had to be married may have been part of some mysterious love debt, or it may just have been a secure way to have "an arrangement" without responsibility or commitment. Bob, who was just one of her current paramours, was buying off his guilt with lavish gifts to both his wife and his lover.

Perhaps Bob liked to talk to me because he needed reassurance that what he was doing was right. Most of his friends had told him he was crazy, but had avoided telling him they themselves had known Andrea on more intimate terms in the past. I never told him anything; I didn't judge him; I didn't tell him he was crazy; I just listened. And I waited.

The next time the black Mercedes interrupted a lawn job, I sat down on the curb to listen and found out he was living in a two-bedroom apartment in a singles complex filled mostly with people half his age. He was, in effect, starting his life over, and the motorcycles on porches, all night-parties, and blasting rock music were reassuring him he was young. But he was beginning to look older.

"I don't know what to do . . . she gets mad 'cause I'm coming over here to see my boys, and yet I know for darn sure she's seeing some guy named Al besides me."

I was a little cruel, but he didn't notice it. "You talking about your wife or your girlfriend?"

"Ah, Mary wouldn't do that; she's too straight. Besides she's got the boys."

"Bob, you think that way because that's the way you need to see Mary as if she were some kind of matronly dullard who would never look at another man. A lot of men find her very interesting, and you'd better get yourself ready to lose her for good."

He thought for a minute. "I know, but with Andrea things are different. Sex is exciting; with Mary it's a dull routine." He waited for me to give him the same sermon everyone else had: how marriage is exciting only if you make it exciting, and so on, but I disappointed him.

"Anything you do the same over the years is supposed to be a routine. The words 'dullness' and 'routine' are simply a negative way of looking at the words 'peaceful' and 'secure'."

His talk stayed on the subject of sex. "Yeah, but Andrea's so good at it." He was smiling stupidly, as if the whole thing were some kind of miracle.

"That's because she's had so much practice." He didn't like the remark and drove off without saying a word. After that the lawn-mowing was a cinch. There were no more curbside consults with a man looking for advice he didn't want.

It's a story that has no end. It's been two years now, and there's been no divorce, Bob's still chasing Andrea and looking for her car in local parking lots, Bob's kids are are still waiting for their Dad to "get well," and Andrea's bills are still getting paid. Bob, the man who thought he was missing something, is still feeling love's hurt after two years, despite banishing the boredom and the routine from his life. He still loves his wife—he says, "I still care for her"—but somehow it sounds shallow and flippant for him to say he loves two women at the same time. His boys could not have been hit with such turmoil at a worse time: young, budding survival plans are suddenly turned upside down; serious love debts are formed that will be paid off by the tears of Bob's sons and daughters-in-law. Mary is bitter, betrayed by the lure of a romantic fantasy that she herself had probably repressed thousands of times out of good judgment and common sense. And Andrea is riding high: she has one more notch in her belt. Her play has run successfully again, and the happy ending for her is that she is once again Daddy's little girl . . . every Daddy's little girl.

Bob's heart and spirit are broken. His friends say, "It's just a mid-life crisis, he'll go back." But Bob is drinking too much now, throwing himself into the "party scene"—the narcotic of broken, and unfulfilled people seeking to ease the pain.

I still think a lot about what happened to them all. Bob had lived a very structured life, never venturing outside his own castle, never expanding the limits of his human loving and giving. If nurturing and caring behavior were ever to have helped him, it would had to have been before Andrea, not after. Bob simply had an ugly case of tunnel vision about the world: didn't everybody make a hundred fifty thousand a year, drive a Mercedes, and have four great kids and a fashionably beautiful wife? He had reached the top of the mountain; he had achieved all the goals he had set for himself. It's tough to be on the top of the mountain and realize it's time to start back down—especially at the age of forty-four.

As I see it, he developed three needs as he approached the top of his mountain. First, he needed to reinforce his sense of virility and strength. Second, he needed to see himself as a physically and emotionally desirable human being. And third, he wanted to be something to somebody besides a meal ticket and a checkbook. Some type of nurturing and caring activity would have done a superb job of answering all three needs. I suppose the blame is mine that I never asked him to get active in Boys Haven. Our society in need is always there; we must not only be willing to act in order to preserve our loving, we must encourage others to nurture with us.

It's a lesson for all of us who are approaching goals we have set: we must continue to set new goals that reinforce our sense of self-strength, our emotional and physical desirability, and our sense of being needed without secondary gain. We must learn to nurture and care for others outside our castles. We must, in sum, set goals that give our lives meaning.

Technology has taken away many of the challenges of staying alive. Romantic ideals promise to take away the rest and to fill the void with "excitement," "fulfillment," and "exotic" experiences. We must be careful to keep our illusions in check. Many fantasies are harmless, but some are very dangerous. I am haunted to this day by the specter of a ten-year-old who watches his father drive away into the night to look for happiness where there is none.

Romantic ideals must be seen for what they are. Otherwise they can be like the Sirens, exotic and alluring, yet beckoning us to dangerous waters and self-destruction.

Questions For Thought

1. *Are there more than three things that you would change about your lover or spouse to improve him or her?*

Loving is the highest form of human acceptance; the correct answer to this question is that there should be no changes desired. This is not realistic but you should be aware of your unrealistic expectation about loving if you want to change more than three things about your lover or spouse.

2. *Do you think anyone is really able to get through life totally free of problems?*

If you answer "yes" to this question, you probably have some unrealistic expectations from loving. Open your eyes, but don't lose your romantic tendencies; you can change them into a form of social idealism that can make your life very fulfilling.

3. *Is there justice for everyone in every situation? Is life fair?*

Again, this question deals with unrealistic expectations from loving and living, but such are the seeds of idealism and social change.

4. *Have you ever been in love with two people at the same time?*

Your romantic expectations may be so complex that no one person can fulfill your needs. People who have excessive dependency needs often find themselves in situations like this. The frustration and confused feelings often lead to self-destructive behavior such as alcohol abuse or compulsive over-eating. The complex needs may be fulfilled by the multiple love relationships, but no real depth or growth is achieved in any of them. The other point not discussed in this chapter is people who are "addicted" to falling in love—the act of emotional immersion into another is so comforting that it is sought out time after time.

The answer is that if you fall in love too much, you need to take your excessive romantic notions and turn them into nurturing and caring behavior. The comforting from the emotional immersion is there without the frustration and confusion.

5. *Can there ever be more than one true love in life?*

If you say "no" you may be an excessive romantic and expect too much from loving. People who are widowed often remarry and have fine relationships. The strength of a love bond is *not* made in heaven; it is made by what the two people in that relationship put into it.

6. *Is there something missing in your love relationship?*

Of course, there may very well be something missing in your relationship that is obvious. The point that should be made in the question is the notion that something is missing but you don't know what it is. Sometimes we can't quite put a finger on what is wrong with our loving, and, if this idea comes up over and over again, you may have excessive romantic expectations.

CHAPTER 14

Play-acting

I've spent a good deal of time talking about the three supporting structures beneath our love relationships: our survival plan—our notion of how loving someone will help us to make it through life; our love debt—our conception of how loving someone will help us to "straighten out" our opinions of the opposite sex and the rest of the world; and our romantic ideal— how, in loving someone, we seek a sense of adventure and excitement to alleviate our boredom and sense of purposelessness. Our love relationships remain "in balance" and pain-free when our unconscious mind perceives these three support beams as intact and in phase.

When stress occurs and upsets this balance, the unconscious mind brings in support to the troubled area by something called "play-acting." "Play-acting" refers to the compensating adjustments we make to our loving to bring the relationship back into balance after stress has knocked it off center. If the desired support is achieved, balance is restored and we feel good again. If the supporting actor in our "play" fails us, our loving falls out of balance and causes us pain. port is achieved, balance is restored and we feel good again. If the supporting actor in our "play" fails us, our loving falls out of balance and causes us pain.

There are several important features of play-acting. First, love hurts when the supporting actors we choose for our plays fail to perform their intended roles, and thus fail to provide us

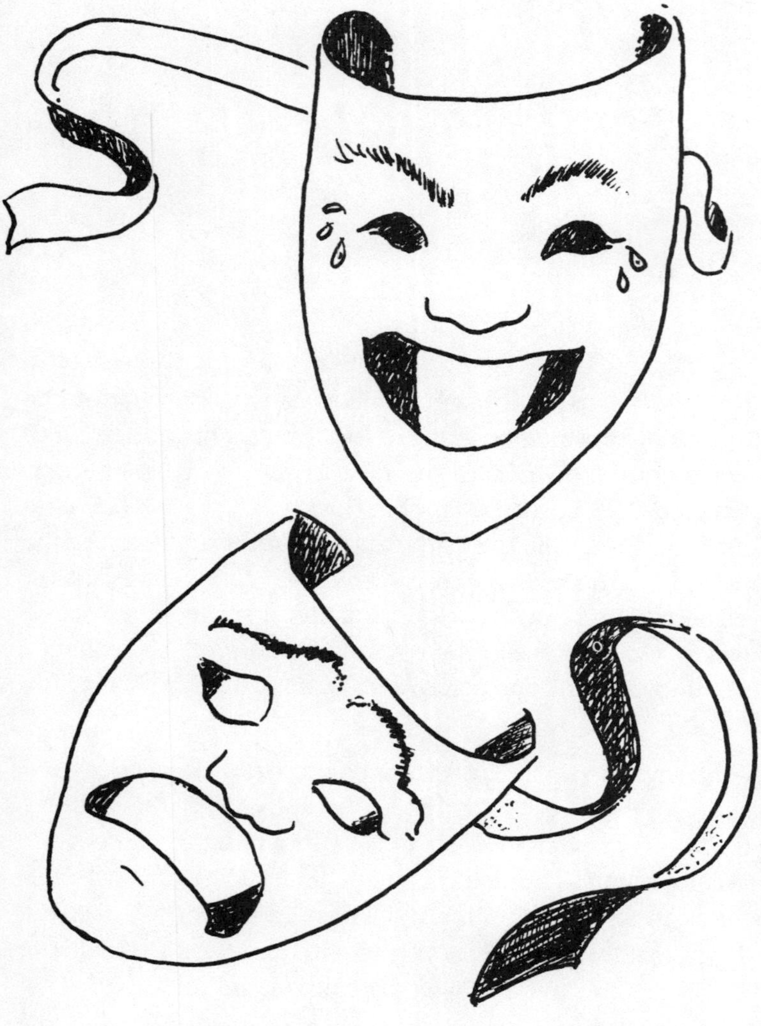

with the help we need. Second, we waste a tremendous amount of emotional energy trying to keep the play running smoothly, and it is this psychic energy, when conserved and stored carefully within us, that gives us our good moods and saves us from slipping into frequent, unexplained depressions. Third, some play-acting succeeds very well in restoring balance to a love relationship, and some fails miserably; the deciding factor is often the strength of the personality and its ability to make the plot real. Fourth, play-acting is an *unconscious* psychic mechanism. In order for it to serve us well, we must make ourselves aware of exactly when we are in a good position to cast people into our little plays. If we allow play-acting to remain hidden from our conscious awareness, then we are at the mercy of plots that may come from conflicts of long ago.

To clarify this point, I am going to limit this discussion to two particular roles that we try to get people to play out for us, focusing on behavior that might be exhibited by someone in these roles.

The two traits that I am going to use as examples for play-acting are "fathering" and "mothering." There are numerous other play-acting traits that we are not going to consider such as: "brother-ing," "sister-ing," "befriend-ing," "ally-ing," "oppos-ing," and so on.

To exhibit "fathering" qualities, we do not have to have gray hair, wear slippers, and read the paper every evening. To exhibit "mothering" qualities, we need not be slightly overweight, wear cotton-print housedresses, or bake cookies all day. These and other stereotyped characteristics may enhance the credibility of the person cast in the role. "Fathering" and "mothering" mean any kind of protective, nurturing, or caring behavior. (We could just as easily call these "parenting" qualities.)

The most obvious example to me of socially acceptable play-acting is the doctor-patient relationship. Here, the doctor is manipulated into "fathering" by social image and patient expectation, and in doing so, counter-manipulates the patient into a childlike role. The same thing occurs when the doctor is a female and is manipulated into a "mothering" role. The doctor enjoys his or her status and power, and the patient enjoys the protection and solicitude.

Unfortunately, none of these roles has anything whatsoever to do with good medical care. The patient who asks a lot of questions or attempts to get involved in the decision-making process may be branded troublesome and is often avoided or sent elsewhere. If we are made aware of this play-acting, which I think neither doctors nor patients really enjoy, then we can alter our approach to seeking medical care and probably get better service.

Another example of play-acting involves the chronically depressed housewife who is tired of playing mother to the whole household, including her husband and pets. Many housewives get themselves into traps like this by overmothering their families, giving too much protection—spoiling them, so to speak, as a means of erasing bad memories. These bad memories are often of the housewife's own mother, who may have been critical, demanding, and non-accepting.

Rather than allow her family to have bad feelings about her the way she had about her mother, the housewife uses too much of her emotional energy catering to the whims and needs of every living thing in the house. She indeed is the "Super-Mom," but the more she acts mothering, the more everybody in the house acts childish, and the more her work load expands. She gets very little emotional support from her husband. A husband who is spoiled by such a catering wife soon loses the knack of giving protection, nurturing, and caring.

In the human species, sharing the emotional support—having the husband "fathering" the wife and the wife "mothering" the husband in equal measure—is a way of keeping both parties

Play-Acting 141

feeling strong and very often is a prerequisite to normal sexual activity.

So the unlucky housewife who finds herself trapped in an over-mothering situation not only is chronically depressed because she uses up all her psychic energy playing "Super-Mom," but also may be sexually deprived. Her husband may be so used to functioning in the child mode that he finds sex uninteresting. This neglect will make her feel unwanted and unacceptable and so the whole cycle begins all over again: she caters to the family, seeking their acceptance and approval.

The only way out of this trap is for the woman to discover why she needs to over-mother: she does not want to see herself as a harsh, critical, demanding mother like her own. She must not suddenly come down hard on the family after making up her mind to change. After all, they are all accustomed to the soft life, and rapid change would only bring cries of protest. Rather, there should be an open family discussion of the problem. Granted, changing her Super-Mom status will require adjustment and flexibility on everyone's part. But once a new pattern of family interaction is established, everyone will benefit.

△　▽　△

When outside stress strikes a love relationship, it's apt to throw the normal, smooth-running interaction out of balance. It does this unless both parties in the relationship have extraordinarily strong pillars of support beneath their loving.

More commonly—but less fortunately—when a relationship is thrown out of balance by stress, the unconscious mind brings in parental play-acting to add support to the weakened areas beneath our loving. The result, as we see in the following two stories, can be a successful return to normal balance in the love relationship, or it can be a snowballing tragedy creating bigger problems than the ones it was intended to solve.

The happier of the two stories is about Cathy, a secretary in her late twenties. As a child, she was very close to her mother, who insisted on the best from her daughter. At times Cathy's mother was a bit critical, but is was clear that Cathy had to "do her part" because so many sacrifices were being made for her. Her mother and father were divorced when Cathy was twelve, and her mother didn't remarry until after the children were grown.

When nineteen-year-old Cathy decided to get married, she had, without realizing it, a shaky view of her own strengths and an enormous sympathy and yearning for men. She viewed her father as a victim in the divorce, and she missed him terribly. Her obvious choice for a husband, then was a *very* fathering character: a strong, domineering, and controlling man, slightly older than herself. What he lacked in understanding and gentleness, he made up for with a strong air of being able to provide for a woman.

The husband had a short temper, however, and a few months after they were married, Cathy realized that her husband was in no way a victim in this marriage, as she had viewed her father in his. After several violent fights with her husband, she felt that she had paid off the love debt of her childhood. She had also quieted her yearning for men who acted fatherly around her, discovering that men who protect and provide aren't necessarily the nicest of people in other ways.

In suffering through this marriage, Cathy amplified her sense of self-strength. If she could survive this, she reasoned, she must have considerable reserves of self-sufficiency. Finding a strong man was no longer necessary or desirable.

Cathy divorced her first husband and married Jim two years later. Jim was a quiet, gentle soul, warm and loving to her. His lack of serious ambition didn't matter. Cathy took advantage of his passive nature to work through a question she still had about her own mothering. Was she, indeed, warm and gentle enough—

and emotionally strong enough—to support both herself and Jim? She answered the question by mothering Jim. She rejoiced with his up-moods; she supported his down-moods; she encouraged him; and she catered to his needs when she wasn't working part-time jobs to supplement the family income. Jim was resilient enough to return the emotional support, although not in the magnitude Cathy provided.

They were both very happy, and they had a baby the following year. Cathy wisely recognized that Jim would have to undergo some "parenting" withdrawal from her when she started to show the baby more attention, and she averted Jim's feelings of being "under-parented" by making Jim take a big role in the care of the baby. This sharing accorded with his warm and gentle nature. Being an actively nurturing father made Jim feel strong, so that Cathy no longer had to provide so much "mothering." The forces in this marriage all seemed to complement one another, and the happiness grew.

The outside stress that threw them off-balance was a fire: it destroyed their small home and put them in dire financial straits. Jim tried to reassure Cathy that everything would soon be all right, but Cathy knew that she would have to get a full-time job for a couple of years to get them back on their feet. She was a fully qualified legal secretary, very good at what she did. Apparently she had picked up some of her mother's stronger, more assertive qualities, and these made her very attractive to prospective employers. She was a pretty girl, and her dress and body language reflected her stability and strength.

Some of the young lawyers who found her attractive made offers she knew were too generous. Her old cravings to be rescued by a kind but strong father-figure began to resurface. It would have been so easy for her to accept a job, an affair, and a temptingly high salary and yet still have her warm and gentle husband at home to mother. Whenever she went for an interview and found herself attracted to a successful, protective, nurturing lawyer, she stopped the play to look for a new leading man.

Cathy finally went to work for an older, successful lawyer who treated her with great kindness and gave her the psychological support she needed. Her salary was not as high as some others had offered, but when she had a problem or a question, she could ask this man and get help without having to worry about incurring a debt. The job was perfect for her. Jim and Cathy were soon back on their feet, and the balance was restored once again in their lives.

Cathy, of course, was totally unaware of the unconscious forces at work in her choosing to extract fathering from a boss. What she knew was that she needed emotional support from a strong male at that time in her life, but that some hidden moral fiber had prevented her from paying for fathering with sex. Thus she had avoided falling back into the trap of her first marriage.

△ ▽ △

If you are happily married and yet find yourself needing emotional support that can't be found at home, you had best return the favor of "parenting" with reciprocal "parenting" rather than say it with your soul and body. To repay someone for coming to your emotional rescue by falling in love with that person (or letting him or her fall in love with you) is a very common danger and may lead to agonizing emotional distress.

It seems fitting to end the first story with such an admonition because reciprocal parenting paid for with an unhealthy love relationship is the basic theme of the second story. It is about Ray, a thirty-eight-year-old businessman who came to therapy under the guise of seeking help with a weight problem. It was obvious that this weight problem wasn't serious, certainly nothing a little racquetball couldn't cure, and I asked him what he hoped to gain by losing a few pounds.

"I've got a few extra pounds because of the booze; you know, with business pressures being what they are, I've been drinking a lot."

This man clearly was not worried about his weight. His drinking had become alarmingly heavy, but I was sure this, too, was only a symptom of something deeper. Yet Ray didn't want to make a full therapy commitment, not because he couldn't afford it or thought it wouldn't help, but because it would make him appear weak to himself.

I was careful to keep the sessions light for a while, using casual talk a lot, so as not to scare him off. Therapy is a humbling experience, and it takes a tremendous amount of strength to admit the need for help. This man obviously didn't have sufficient strength, and I didn't feel it would be productive to rub his nose in his weakness by going through a lot of the formalities of the therapeutic commitment.

Instead I asked him if he was happy with his wife.

"A man couldn't ask for a better gal. She puts up with so much from me. But we're loving and warm, and we have everything we want. . . . I guess that's what makes me feel guilty . . . "

He knew that I understood. I said, as matter-of-factly as I could, "You fool around on her a lot?"

He must have felt comfortable enough by now to open up about the situation. "I have everything I want, I'm happy, I love my wife, and yet when I see a good-looking girl, I lose my common sense and start putting the make on her . . . nothing heavy, just small talk, but I *know* that I'm trying to get her into the sack, and that's usually where it ends up."

He spoke with genuine sincerity, as if he had some kind of rare disease. He felt alone and was hurting over behavior he clearly enjoyed on the one hand, but didn't understand on the other.

He went on, "And it's not as though I need a mistress, or something steady that I don't get at home. The sex at home is great. When I meet a girl, I feel like I'm really falling for her. After we've made love a few times, and believe me, it's always great, I find myself falling for someone else. I still care about the first girl, but the sex doesn't interest me any more, and the whole cycle starts over again. The girls I let go of get mad, and keep calling me. I'm running in circles trying to keep everybody happy. I'm really afraid my wife's gonna' catch me, and it'll be all over for me."

He told me that his drinking was not just partying on the sly, but escape drinking to shield him from the turmoil in his life that he couldn't seem to get rid of. I gently asked the question that would let him talk about his parents without making it seem like he was in deep psychotherapy.

" . . . did your father fool around a lot?"

"Nah. My old man was too straight. I mean, he went right by the book. He was super-strict with my brother and me . . . the whole family was afraid of him, even the dog. But, you know, he was a good-hearted Joe; he wasn't exactly gentle, but he'd take the shirt off his back for you."

Ray continued the story about his parents and siblings and unknowingly painted a fairly vivid picture of his survival plan and a significant love debt. His father's criticisms had left Ray questioning his own ability to be a success in life. This insecurity had made Ray particularly vulnerable to stresses about money. The blueprint in Ray's mind did not allow him to seek reassurance about survival (money) from his father, who, through the process of incorporation, had become Ray himself. In other words, when Ray worried about anything, his father's criticisms of long ago frightened him out of thinking that he (Ray) could take care of the problem. Yet Ray was a survivor, and he quickly became conditioned to finding reassurances about his worries in other people.

The rest of Ray's early view of the world had, of course, come from his mother, who was a warm person, but who had appeared weak in comparison to the father. Ray was the younger of the two boys, and when he sought solace from his mother, she clearly did not come through as well as she had for the first child. This is a fairly typical pattern: by the time the second or third child comes along, mom has more confidence in her abilities as a mother, and has less time to devote to catering to these later arrivals. This "benign neglect" can make these kids more self-sufficient and ambitious, but also more competitive for the nurturing attentions of women later in life.

When Ray reached late adolescence, he was inadequately outfitted psychologically to feel comfortable facing life's troubles. When anything worried him, he would feel his fears of inadequacy start to emerge, and he would seek someone else for emotional support. If he found a man, it was great; an alliance was formed and the necessary support was reciprocated in a mutually beneficial relationship. (In fact, Ray had formulated his business around a partnership not so much for financial reasons, but for the emotional support his partner afforded him.)

In situations where there were no men to help, however, Ray naturally turned to women, and there were plenty of those in his daily travels. But interacting with these women on an emotional basis didn't seem to be enough for him. It was as if he were a child again, competing with his older brother for the attentions of their mom. He needed to possess his woman totally, and to him this meant everything—including marriage, if necessary. He had a history of three bad marriages and innumerable relationships. He was now in his fourth marriage, and he seemed to have settled down a bit—at least in terms of getting married.

Ray initiated his relationships with the women he hoped would lend him support by using play-acted parenting traits as the bait. The women who would find him attractive and invariably end up in a relationship with him were the mirror-image of his love debt profile. Ray incorporated strong, protective traits from his father, and projected the image of a fathering male, even though Ray himself had a poor sense of self-strength. These feelings of self-weakness were hidden in his unconscious, and, in fact, Ray's "macho" attempts at fathering were loud denials of the rumblings coming up from below.

In addition to this, Ray yearned for the emotional approval of women; again, this was a feeling he had carried from childhood, having constantly sought the attentions of a weak and tired mother. The women in his life had incorporated strong, nurturing traits from their mothers, and projected images of mothering females. They did this in spite of their own unconscious lack of self-strength (which was, like Ray's, denied loudly by unusually assertive behavior). They were also yearning for contact with fathering males, a yearning that stemmed from their own absent or ineffective fathers.

It was truly reciprocal, play-acted parenting. When Ray or his women felt stress, they sought emotional support from parenting people of the opposite sex; but as they played for keeps, the price for such support was falling painfully into and out of love.

Two questions come to mind about Ray and his women. First, why did they have to be so intensely involved, including sexual play—why not just be friends who shared problems? Second, why were Ray's relationships outside his marriage so fleeting and short-lived?

I've already partially answered the first question: Ray needed to possess these women totally in order to do away with his fears that his needs might not get primary consideration from the women with whom he interacted. This anxiety was translated into a full-scale sexual relationship. After all, a friend could on occasion refuse emotional support, but a lover would never put her own needs first.

Another answer that would explain the intensity of Ray's relationships is that people who seek parenting in the form of nurturing and support do not like to share their source. Just so, Ray had felt in childhood that in order to get his mother's undivided attention, he had to upstage his older brother.

The intensity of Ray's relationships could also be explained by the fact that men who have had somewhat harsh and unaffectionate fathers often try to overcome their own tendencies to be hard-hearted, and perhaps overact the role of the currently fashionable "sensitive male." Ray's attempts to be sensitive and to

Play-Acting

hide his critical, demanding side were, of course, very attractive to the women he tried to "father," and served to intensify the relationships.

The answer to the second question, why Ray's relationships were so short-lived, lies in the hidden weaknesses of the women themselves. Ray's primary motivation in play-acting the parent role towards women was to possess them for their strength and support. When these women finally submitted, they were, in effect, submitting to Ray's protection and nurturing as a replacement parent-figure. In this submission, they were allowed, so to speak, to let their weakness come out. This is precisely why they sought Ray's fathering. After two or three interplays, the woman were basking in the warmth of Ray's pretend fathering, letting the weak, vulnerable parts of their personalities heal from the wounds of needing male support for so long.

At this point the women had stopped being the strong, mothering females that Ray had originally sought. No longer supportive, they were now burdens; the additional stress spurred Ray to look for another make-believe "mother" figure to take away the awful feeling that the world was closing in on him.

This is what brought Ray to seek help: the world was indeed closing in. The stress that had triggered the last burst of "falling in love" was that his business partner wanted to sell out and leave Ray to run the enterprise all alone. Ray quickly became full of free-floating stress, and, at the time he came for therapy, was involved with three different women besides his wife. The guilt, the hiding, the time-juggling, the phone calls, and the drinking were more than he could take.

When he finally admitted his need for help, it wasn't a moment too soon. He was a very tired person, indeed.

Questions For Thought

1. *Do the arguments and fights in your love relationships seem inappropriately intense?*

This indicates that you may be really fighting about something hidden in your childhood? Your spouse or lover may "spark" certain unconscious images and end up paying for the sins of your parent of the opposite sex.

2. *Are you obssessed with your lover's "past"?*

Most therapists agree that this painful problem is caused by a poor sense of self-worth, and, of course, the "nurture-cure" suggested in this book will help tremendously. But some obsession with a lover's past could be the result of play-acting: a painful rejection of a parent of the opposite sex or even a remembrance of early sibling rivalry.

3. *Do you get a little uneasy or angry inside when you come home and your spouse isn't there?*

This could be more play-acting. If there is no good reason for your anger, you could be unconsciouly "remembering" some wrong, however insignificant, done to you by your parent of the opposite sex.

4. *Try to think of all the people in your life that you've had intense feelings for (include teenage "crushes"). Do you notice that half of these are the exact opposite in physical traits as the other half (tall, blond vs. short, dark, etc.)?*

If you notice this to be true, you may notice that one half of your loves were physically similar to your parent of the opposite sex (limit your criteria to height and coloring). If this is the case, you may be play-acting in your love relationships. This is not so unhealthy in itself, but it can be very painful if the plot is not played out correctly. The exact opposite choices you made served two purposes: first, they totally did away with any incestuous fears you may have developed; they were simply your way of trying a totally different actor in order to get a different ending.

Play-Acting

5. *If you have pictures of the people in #4 above, try this experiment: use tracing paper to outline their jawlines, hairlines, cheekbones, lower lips, and noses. See if you notice any similarities or patterns. Now trace an early picture of your parent of the opposite sex. Compare the tracings.*

It may be stretching a bit, but often the results of this little experiment are startling. Physical similarity to the person remembered makes the plot more believable.

6. *Are you unusually jealous?*

Jealousy is usually linked to a poor sense of self-worth and to guilt and suspicion projected onto the lover. Yet some aspects of jealousy can be linked to play-acting and the love debt. A man who feels "under-nurtured" by his mother may be very jealous of the time his wife spends away from him. He may cover up and justify his jealousy by "accusing" her of being unfaithful.

7. *Have you broken up and reconciled with a lover or a spouse several times?*

In addition to being a strong model of the parent of the opposite sex, your lover or spouse may also be helping you with a very strong love debt. If the insights gained in this book don't get you off this merry-go-round, you should seek the services of a kind and non-judgemental therapist.

8. *Do you always seem to pick the same kind of lover?*

This indicates that you probably are trying to play act away some very painful conflict or disappointment from your past dealings with your parent of the opposite sex. The most vivid example is the woman with an alcoholic father who almost without fail falls in love with men who drink too much (or have the emotional raw material to do so) in hopes of "changing them."

9. *Do you flirt more when you are under stress?*

Flirting is a natural way to concretize images of a fond parent of the opposite sex. This new living image brings back secure feelings from childhood and the stress goes away.

The problems arise when this process is mistaken for "true love" and the feelings are pursued with destructive action.

CHAPTER 15

The Essence of Nurturing and Caring

Throughout this book, I've told you about many things that make love hurt. The stories may have seemed severe, perhaps even exaggerated, but basically they've been true. I hope, in all the plots, subplots, and case studies, you've seen bits and pieces of your own suffering if for no other reason than to realize that you are not alone.

But what about this prescription I've given you to take away your pain, this prescription for nurturing and caring behavior as a therapy form? What is it? What should you do *When Love Hurts?*

To help you understand what nurturing and caring behavior is and how it can help you, I'm going to tell you a little about what it *isn't*.

Even though nurturing behavior is going to elevate your self-perspective and expand you basic humanity, the motives behind your caring must never be selfish, or the therapeutic benefit will be lost. You must have good motives behind your good works. The businessman who donates money to a local charity only after he phones his advertising agency for a press release is unquestionably sincere in his motive to improve his image in the

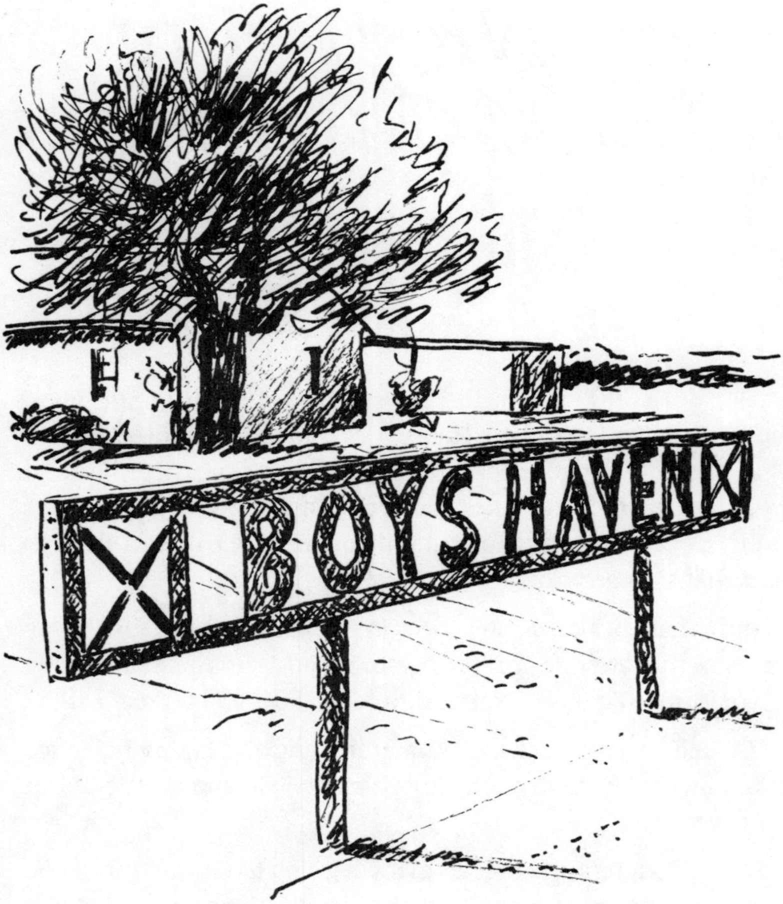
BOYS HAVEN

community, but the obvious secondary gain erases any chance of improving his image in his own eyes.

Indeed, if we consider him in light of the human condition of getting up in the morning, trying to make a living, and waiting to die, then his strengthening of his business at the expense of himself only makes his cycle more of a trap.

Every force has its antithesis, its opposite but equal reaction, and nurturing and caring seems to be the opposite of something I call "predator-victim" thinking and behavior. It is the product of certain tendencies which have evolved with us throughout the ages, and it is progressively moving toward becoming a cult in our society. The more frightened we get about becoming victims, the more determined we get to become predators. It's the "get them before they get me" philosophy; it is really an outgrowth of our primitive, animal-like instincts to kill or be killed. It's not just a case of bad people hurting innocent people; rather it is a case of people who are neither truly bad nor entirely good having the *ability* to hurt someone if provoked. And we seem to be provoking one another more and more lately.

Predator-Victim thinking and behavior is seen in all kinds of relationships, even love relationships. In society, it may be so whitewashed and overlaid with socially acceptable behavior as to be unrecognizable. Yet it is a pervasive, growing force that is undermining our ability to love properly, and the only sure eradicator of this demon is nurturing and caring.

So what is nurturing and caring, this thinking and behavior that I've said can help your love relationships and even other day-to-day interaction? Loving is, by nature, an agreement of trust. If you feel any vulnerability in a love relationship, such an agreement is not going to work very well for you. If you feel weak when you love, and if you happen to get hurt, you will probably strike back. This emotional vengeance snowballs into a way of life in which many people are hopelessly trapped.

So for this prescription to work for you, it must erase some of your vulnerability in loving and give you a sense of strength. Nurturing, then, is not so much an action or situation as it is an *attitude,* an attitude of your strength. It is an approach that you should transform into action when you see that your relationship to the rest of the world is not going well. In particular, when love hurts, you can bolster your sense of self-strength by acknowledging the existence of society's victims and laying hands upon their wounds. Like Doubting Thomas, you must see and feel the pain of others if you are ever to be whole yourself.

All too often we lose perspective on good works. We revere the great heart surgeons who hold life in their gloved hands, the scientific daredevils who brave new frontiers, yet we take for granted the unexpected kindness of a bus driver who smiles at us on a rainy Monday morning. All great acts of heroism and small acts of kindness sit side by side in the universe and, from the top of the cosmos, may well appear the same.

When we see ourselves in relation to others who need us, therein lies our perception of self-strength. I feel certain that the inborn human trait of solicitude toward others is an evolutionary progress toward a higher life form, and that the growth toward that life form holds not just a perception of strength, but strength itself.

How Do We Change The Way We Care

Nurturing and Caring as a healing form for your love relationships embodies certain practical considerations. I am going to list four of them and then spend a little time describing each.

Nurturing and Caring is:

1. . . . constantly quieting the predator side of us.

2. . . . an attitude of kindness and gentleness.

3. . . . an attitude of forgiveness and acceptance.

4. . . . choosing to be needed.

Quieting the Predator

Men seem to have a special problem developing a nurturing attitude because of the stereotype laid upon them by society: they are the protectors of the family unit. The idea that men should be laden with most of the predator qualities of the species is certainly not handed down phylogenetically. The female of many species is not only the defender of the family unit, but often hunts and kills for food. So until the sexual stereotypes of our species die out, men will have to risk their "macho" image, quiet the predator instinct, and become more gentle in their attitudes and interactions with others outside their protective domain.

As you will see in the Appendix, however, much of the nurturing and caring activity in society has been specifically structured for men with the idea of promoting community involvement tied in with family activity. I am thinking specifically of activities like Little League coaching, Rotary Clubs, Optimist Clubs, the Elks, the Eagles, the Moose and many other civic-minded organizations which, through their fund-raising events, nurture the less fortunate in society.

Yet we must all recognize that we have the demon of predator-victim thinking lurking somewhere within us, and to effectively become nurturing in character, we must quiet this baser side of our nature. The effects of this demon on our behavior toward the world may very well be subtle; in fact, the most common manifestation of this is *neglect*.

Predator-victim thinking tells us that we are either to be predators or victims. Most of us are not so self-serving that we do everything for secondary gain. And so the reason we might neglect to help someone, in however small a way, is not that we aren't getting paid, but that we just don't want to become victims. Because of the fear engendered by predator-victim thinking, we respond to the needs of others with neglect.

Thinking about men denying their predator side and getting active in nurturing behavior reminded me of my neighbor Bud. He came over Saturday morning to ask me if I was going to sponsor another billboard for the Sugar Creek Little League. I asked him why he stayed active in kids' baseball even though his sons were too old. He told me some things that I thought I should pass on to you.

Bud sat back in a living room chair, took a sip of coffee, and said, "It's funny, you know, I thought after the boys got out that I'd quit too, but things just seem to go better with me when I'm coaching. Sure, I feel needed, but it's not so much that as I feel *important*. I'm a source of strength and direction to the kids. Most of them look up to me, even ask me for advice . . . they fill some strange void and even do things my own kids didn't do. The strangest thing is that Janie and I get along better when I'm coaching; she's a little sharp sometimes but it seems to roll off my back. I guess that's because I feel important and needed . . . like I'm 'walking tall.' I just don't worry as much either."

Bud and Janie had bypassed all the trouble that usually hits marriages after fifteen or twenty years. Bud realized that feeling important and strong not only made him unafraid of the predators in society but of the sometimes intense assertiveness of his own life. His work with the kids gave him a sense of self-power that enabled him to function in his marriage on an equal level with his wife.

△ ▽ △

Attitude of Kindness and Gentleness
To make love not hurt and develop a nurturing character, you must perceive yourself as a kind and gentle person. If you perceive yourself as abrasive and rude in dealing with people (or in fact act that way), then you will surely carry some of this behavior into your love relationships. Kindness and gentleness must be practiced over and over or you will lose your touch.

Simple gestures toward people you encounter every day are a wonderful way to start. If you deal with the public, for example, make an effort to be patient and friendly, to listen and respond wholeheartedly. As in a love relationship, people will perceive your kindness and gentleness as qualities to be emulated. If you can make this simple beginning, then the more heroic forms of self-dedication will come easy for you. If you program yourself to act kindly and gently with people, you will make a better lover. You must remember Ronnie, the patient who treated people just as he was treated. Give kindness and gentleness in any relationship, and you will receive it.

△   ▽   △

I recently had the opportunity to see Elizabeth, my neighbor in the story. How time had flown by! John had graduated from high school and was working as a welder earning good money. Walter, the sixteen-year-old boy in the story, was now twenty-three and still in contact with Mark. The two visited often and traded stories. Elizabeth said that Mark was a changed man since he had met Walter: "I never thought my husband would change, but his friendship with Walter seemed to tone Mark down. He used to charge around like an untamed bull when he was mad, but I guess Walter, being sensitive and all, has gotten Mark used to being gentler with people, especially me."

Mark had learned the art of kindness and gentleness from a strange symbiotic relationship with someone just like himself and transferred those qualities into his marriage. It was something that begging from his wife, counseling, reading books, and listening to advice from his friends couldn't accomplish.

An Attitude of Forgiveness and Acceptance

One of the most difficult changes that you will encounter in developing a nurturing attitude is the art of forgiveness and acceptance in living and loving. The reason is your inborn need for a sense of justice, and society has insidiously preached the message that vengeance is a form of justice. Because of this, vengeance, even in its simplest form, feels good.

Of course, you are well aware that vengeance solves nothing. And every act of "getting even" is basically destructive to yourself and to your evolution toward higher forms of human interaction, especially in love relationships. If you can succeed in reducing your needs to "get even," and practice the art of acceptance, you will certainly enjoy the benefits of a sense of self-worth that will far overshadow the offenses of any predator.

Choosing to be Needed

The most concrete way to develop a nurturing and caring attitude and thus improve the way that you see yourself is to actually get involved in the needs of others. To get involved in the more active forms of nurturing and caring, you must first survey the needs in your immediate community and then find a situation to match your preferences and time schedule. This is very often the major stumbling point to getting involved in community needs because it is more easily said than done. For this reason, I have included a rather complete, step-by-step Appendix for a simple approach to getting involved in community work and thus living the nurturing and caring way.

A greater stumbling point is the embarrassment you might feel in calling a place and asking if they need your help. A few techniques for calling and setting up a program that will suit you are outlined in the Appendix, but very often embarrassment and fear of looking for the needs of the community have their origin in doubt, doubt as to whether the activity will do any good in making you feel better.

The Essence of Nurturing and Caring

Testimony to the effectiveness of nurturing and caring is hard to come by. People just don't talk about it much, they just do it.

You must know people like this. They seem happier, more fulfilled, and little in life seems to get to them. Problems in their love relationships are never mentioned in casual talk, probably because personal relationships take a back seat to personal fulfillment, and this makes loving more a choice of joy than a need to survive.

Anna, the girl who wanted the courage to divorce her husband, summed it up very well one night when I saw her in a local club still very married and seemingly happy with her husband. She came over, put her arm around my shoulder, and thanked me for pushing her into the volunteer program at Green Pines Nursing Center. She ran a wheelchair exercise program two hours a week; the entire thing was her design—I had only suggested a nurturing project to help her with her unsettled feelings about her husband. The magic had worked.

"It's strange," she said, "I thought the people who helped out in places like that were special—you know, church groups and all—but most of the people who volunteer got started just like me . . . embarrassed and scared. I never thought a couple hours a week could be so important to my whole attitude about living. Watching their faces, feeling them squeeze my hand and not letting go . . . makes me glad I was born."

I suppose there are thousands of projects I could tell you about. I hope you find one for yourself that you like, and one that will elevate the perspective of life by nurturing and caring.

I once knew a man who had a very special secret. He certainly never told anyone about it; I heard it from a jail guard who was a patient of mine. Every Saturday this man went down to the county jail, the place full of the truly poor in spirit, the losers in society, and he brought a candy bar and a pack of cigarettes to each man. He simply reached through the bars and said, "Hi, this is for you," and shook hands. He must have flabbergasted the inmates.

We can never know the full effect of such a tiny measure of kindness, but surely it sits in the cosmos, gnawing away at the demon.

APPENDIX

It would be very helpful if I could give you a complete list of the opportunities to get involved in the needs of others, but such a list is impossible because so many projects are endemic to single communities. Yet the volunteer opportunities almost always have a generic structure behind them, and have different names in different cities. For instance, Boys Haven, Boys Harbour, Boys Hollow, and Boys Town are all names of community-supported homes for boys in various places.

As you look through the following list, you will be astounded at the sheer number of different places that you can learn to nurture and care. It's not so important what you choose, but only that you choose an activity that you really enjoy. It's important that you never dread going to your particular volunteer project. If this happens for whatever reason, it's time to find another activity.

From my own experience and that of my patients and friends, I've found that two hours a week is an optimum amount of time to spend in therapeutic nurturing. You should pick two hours on a day when you aren't pressed for time, and, if possible, use time that you might ordinarily waste, like watching a TV show you don't particularly enjoy.

The first real step to getting started is to survey your community to find out just what kind of structured nurturing situations are available. As you become more at ease doing volunteer work, you will automatically structure your nurturing activities after things and around people you like. Until then, however, it's best to start this new venture is a structured environment.

There are a few ways to find out what's available where you live. Read over the following list and then consult the "Yellow Pages" of your local phone directory under "Social Services Organizations." You might also find a "Volunteer" column in your local newspaper—they often have titles like "Volunteer Action," "Volunteer Vista," and "Volunteer Voice." Talk to your friends and acquaintances on a casual basis and see if they've heard of any particular situation which might interest you. Talking to people sets you up for the next step in getting involved—finding a partner or partners.

There is strength in numbers; finding a friend with whom you can begin this venture will make it fun and ease some of the initial fears. A partner is not so important if you're going to join an established organization like the Optimists or the various women's clubs.

After you've dialed the phone, what you need to say is very simple: "I've got a little extra time, and I'd like to do some volunteer work for you. Can you give me some information?" If they don't need your help (a rarity), they'll send you to someone who does need it. Organizations need volunteers; they appreciate you and they always show it.

Children as Objects of Nurturing

Children are especially likely candidates for nurturing: there is no better way to improve our sense of self-strength than to become a Super-Parent. Indeed, much of the structured volunteer work is centered on kids.

- Girl and Boy Scout Troops
- Campfire Girls
- Boys Club

Appendix

- Big Brother Programs
- YMCA and YWCA
- Day Care Centers
- Church Activities (such as Mothers' Day Off)
- Little League
- Child Abuse Centers
- Foster Home Programs
- Hospital Volunteer Work on Pediatric Wards
- Orphanages
- Special Olympics
- Crippled Children Summer Camps (often sponsored by local March of Dimes or Muscular Dystrophy Association)
- Information and Referral Center of the United Way
- your local Mental Health Association (Starting Point to get involved with Special Children)
- Red Cross
- Salvation Army
- local Family Services Association

There may even be some kids in your neighborhood who enjoy talking to you. Sometimes it's difficult to stop yardwork to talk to a youngster, but the effect of kind patience on a developing personality can be long-lived. Interaction between adults and children is a natural form of nurturing.

Adults as Objects of Nurturing

- Church activities
- Nursing Homes (most are desperately in need of volunteers—they will structure a program for you or let you make one up)

- Family Crisis Centers (includes abuse victims and shelter programs)
- Suicide Prevention Centers
- Goodwill Industries
- local offices of Mental Health and Rehabilitation
- Alcoholic Treatment Centers and Alcoholics Anonymous
- Community Action Committees
- Animal Shelters
- Rape Crisis Centers
- Red Cross
- Mothers Against Drunk Drivers
- Salvation Army
- United Way
- hospices
- county jails and prisons
- Halfway Houses for emotionally handicapped adults
- Senior Citizens Activity Centers

There are probably many wonderful opportunities to practice the "nurture cure" in your own community that I've left out. Find them and enrich your life!

When suffering and misfortune strike, some of us feel forsaken by our Creator. But the Force of our Creation lives within our human spirit and we must let It out.

As Elizabeth wanted to tell John that Christmas Eve, "There are no knights-in-shining-armor on white horses . . . . " There are only people like us.

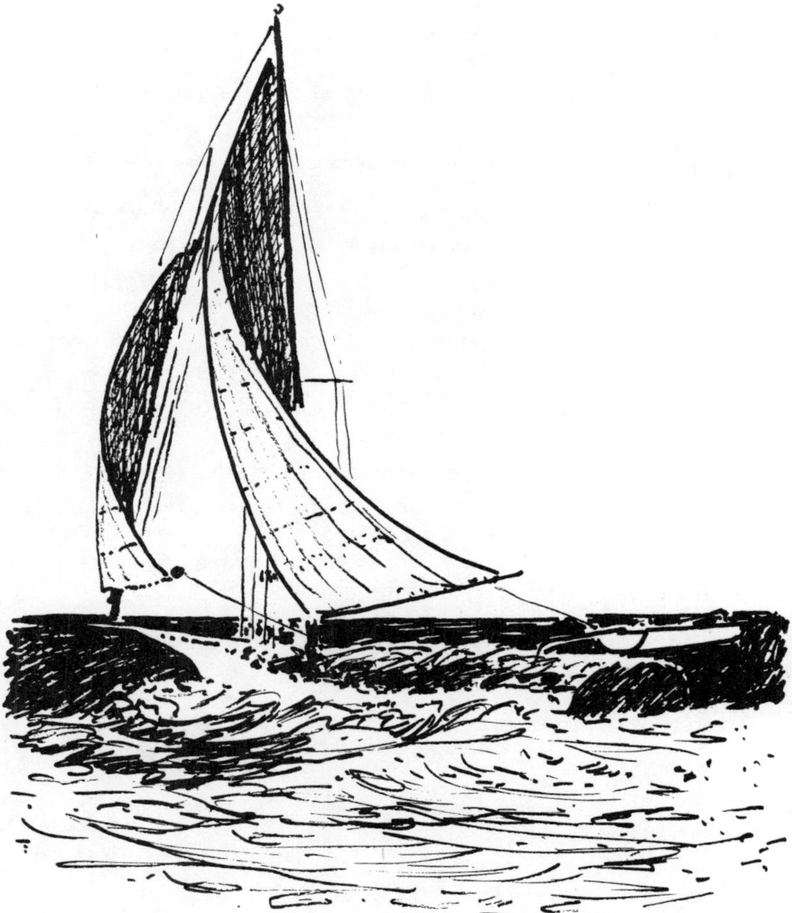

The Love Debt

	Romantic Type of Love Debtor	*Practical Type of Love Debtor*
FOR WOMEN — Mother may be:	• loud-mouthed • assertive • critical and demanding • cold, rejecting • emotionally abusive to your father • domineering • bad guy	• victim • good guy • passive and meek • afraid of your father • refuge of kindness for you in times of trouble • one who did all the work and got no reward
Father may be:	• driven off by your mother • meek and quiet • sweet and lovable • good guy • always praising you • generous	• sexually abusive • physically abusive to your mother • bad guy • cold, rejecting • self-serving

	Romantic Type of Love Debtor	*Practical Type of Love Debtor*
Your Behavior Pattern As a Love Debtor May Be:	• romantic, in love with love • approval-seeking to the opposite sex • taking blame rather than fighting; peacemaker • martyr • affectionate, passionate • getting along well with the opposite sex • often a victim in love relationships yourself	• practical, self-serving • often unemotional, logical • sometimes insensitive • sex often lacks tenderness, foreplay and may even seem vengeful • plenty of friends of the same sex; you may behave differently in front of opposite sex

The Love Debt

FOR MEN

	Romantic Type of Love Debtor	Practical Type of Love Debtor
Mother may be:	• victim • good guy • passive parent • afraid of • the parent you always ask for money • buffer between you and your father	• domineering • shrewish • argumentative • cold, rejecting • sick or absent • emotionally abusive to your father
Father may be:	• stern, disciplinarian • bad guy • one everybody was afraid of • the decision-maker for the family • physically abusive	• passive • henpecked • deceased • unable to make sound decisions • physically small • unassertive with your mother

	Romantic Type of Love Debtor	Practical Type of Love Debtor
Your Behavior Pattern As a Love Debtor May Be:	• romantic, in love with love • approval-seeking to the opposite sex • taking blame rather than fighting; peacemaker • martyr • affectionate, passionate • getting along well with the opposite sex • often a victim in love relationships yourself	• practical, self-serving • often unemotional, logical • sometimes insensitive • sex often lacks tenderness, foreplay and may even seem vengeful • plenty of friends of the same sex; you may behave differently in front of opposite sex

Suggested Further Reading

Arthur, Julietta K., *Retire to Action*, Abingdon Press: 1969.

Bach, George K. & Laura Torbet, *A Time For Caring*, Delacorte: 1982.

Buckley, Marie, *Breaking Into Prison,* Beacon Press: 1974.

Carkhuff, Robert R., *Helping and Human Relations: A Primer for Lay and Professional Helpers*, Holt, Rinehart & Winston: 1969.

Crook, William H., *Warrior for the Poor*, Morrow: 1969.

DeSilva, Benjamin & Richard Lucas, *A Practical School Volunteer and Teacher Aide Program*, Parker Press: 1974.

Frankl, Viktor E., *Man's Search for Meaning*, Beacon Press: 1959.

Fromm, Erich, *Man For Himself*, Holt, Rinehart & Winston: 1947.

Fromm, Erich, *To Have Or To Be*, Harper and Row: 1976.

Gordon, Janet G., *The Volunteer Powerhouse*, Rutledge Press: 1982.

Greer, Virginia, *Emergency*, Christian Herald Book: 1977.

Kraines, Samuel H., *Live and Help Live*, MacMillan: 1951.

Lobb, Charlotte, *Exploring Careers Through Volunteerism*, Richard Rosen Press: 1976.

McGill, Michael E., *Changing Him, Changing Her*, Simon and Shuster: 1982.

Messer, Alfred A., "Continuation in Adult Life of Parent-Child Relationships: the Effect on Marriage," *Medical Aspects of Human Sexuality*, XVII, No. 1, Nov. '83.

Index

Approval-seeking behavior, 62, 65, 77, 78, 96, 109, 121, 122, 124

Boys Haven, 14, 51, 66, 72, 81, 95, 134, 163

Changing, 27, 31–36, 53, 67, 73, 98, 113, 114, 135, 159
Cycles, 42, 55, 155

Incorporation, 108–110, 147, 148

Love and pain, 9–14, 29, 36, 37–38, 75, 89, 96, 125, 133, 153, 155, 158

Love debt, 11, 40, 42, 69, 74–78, 107–124, 125, 129, 130, 132, 133, 137, 142, 146, 147, 168–169
 practical, 78, 108, 110, 110, 111, 121, 123, 124, 168–169
 romantic, 108, 109, 110, 111, 120, 123, 168–169
Love Pyramid, 11, 39-41. See *Survival Plan, Love Debt, Romantic Ideal.*

Nurturing and caring, 9, 11–13, 19–23, 36, 39, 66, 74–78, 91, 94, 95–96, 100, 118, 120, 121, 134, 148, 149, 150, 153–162, 163–165

Parallels, 26–27, 29, 73, 100

Patterns, 9–11, 21, 25–29, 96, 11
Perspectives on loving, 17–23, 36, 120
Play-acting, 130, 137–152
   actors, 53, 116, 117
   play, 67, 78, 88, 116, 118, 130
   plot, 42, 86, 88, 95, 117, 130
   roles, 9, 32, 39, 86, 87, 130
   script, 53, 86, 89
Power, 35–36, 107, 121
Predator-victim thinking, 40, 98–99, 107–110, 111, 112, 113, 115, 117, 120, 121, 122, 127, 129, 142, 156, 157, 158

Romantic Ideal, 11, 40–42, 75–77, 125–136, 137

Self-image, self-perception, 21, 22, 27, 33–36, 40, 42, 78, 87, 115, 118, 119, 121, 153
Self-strength, 89, 95–96, 121, 134, 142, 147, 156, 165
Storm and calm, 55, 56, 67, 71–78
Survival Plan, 11, 40, 42, 53, 59–64, 75, 78, 85–105, 109, 111, 112, 115, 125, 127, 130, 133, 137, 146

Other Books of Interest to You

Big & Beautiful
How to Be Gorgeous on Your Own Grand Scale
by Ruthanne Olds

A brand new way for large women to dress and to feel about themselves. Learn to dress better not thinner, reflecting your personal style in the most becoming way. Discover the secrets of successful big models and learn how you can "make it big" in this new career.

200 pages, 8×9, color photos and illustrations
$8.95 quality paper

Bringing Up Parents
The Adolescent's Handbook
by Alex J. Packer

If you are not getting along with your parents, teenagers. If you are not getting along with your teenager, parents—here's help. Instead of telling parents in highly technical terms how to raise their children this book tells kids, in their own language, how to "bring up" their parents. Kids learn the skills of getting along with and motivating people to help their parents learn to trust them, let them make their own mistakes, listen to what they say, and respect their opinions.

250 pages, 8×9, cartoon illustrations
$8.95 quality paper

Choices of a Growing Woman
by Maggie S. Davis

A woman-to-woman testimony to the author's belief that a woman can always choose to start moving in directions that feel better. "A sparkling gem, filled with wisdom—honest, personal. It asked all the right questions and touched me deeply. In fact, Maggie Davis makes 'growing' contagious," praised Nena O'Neill, author of *Shifting Gears* and *The Marriage Promise*.

144 pages, 5×8
$4.95 quality paper

Couples: The Art of Staying Together
by Anita and Robert Taylor, M.D.

"A provocative study that will help people enhance the quality of their couple relationships," said Mel Krantzler, *Learning to Love Again*. And that's what this book does: it takes eight very different couples as case studies and explores how they interact and what benefits they get from being together to help you keep your relationship strong...or get it back together.

211 pages, 6×9
$7.95 hardcover/$4.95 quality paper

Win the Happiness Game
by Dr. William G. Nickels

A step-by-step personal development program that shows you how to schedule happiness in your life, discover joy, express love openly, develop self-reliance and self-support, conquer your fears, worries and doubts. "I am impressed by *Win the Happiness Game*, the unique and practical book by Dr. William Nickels."
—Dr. Norman Vincent Peale

183 pages, 6×9
$6.95 quality paper

Available at your local booksellers!
Or send check plus $1.50 postage & handling to:
ACROPOLIS BOOKS LTD.
2400 17th St., N.W., Washington, D.C. 20009